Green Roofs and Rooftop Gardens

Beth Hanson and Sarah Schmidt

Editors

BROOKLYN
BOTANIC
GARDEN

Elizabeth Peters
DIRECTOR OF DIGITAL
AND PRINT MEDIA

Sarah Schmidt
SENIOR EDITOR

Dr. Susan Pell
SCIENCE EDITOR

Joni Blackburn
COPY EDITOR

Elizabeth Ennis
ART DIRECTOR

Scot Medbury
PRESIDENT

Elizabeth Scholtz
DIRECTOR EMERITUS

Handbook #198

Copyright © 2012 by Brooklyn Botanic Garden, Inc.

ISBN 978-1-889538-81-5

Printed in China by Ocean Graphics Press.

♻ Printed with soy-based inks on
postconsumer recycled paper.

Guides for a Greener Planet are published by
Brooklyn Botanic Garden, 1000 Washington Avenue,
Brooklyn, NY 11225.

Learn more at bbg.org/handbooks.

Cover: The green roof of the United States Postal Service's Morgan Distribution Center in Manhattan. Above: Green roofs are especially popular on recently constructed residential towers in the Manhattan neighborhood of Battery Park City, thanks to sustainable building policies enacted by the local development authority.

Green Roofs and Rooftop Gardens

Greening the Fifth Façade
Beth Hanson

Traditional black tar and asphalt roofs are affordable, watertight, and ubiquitous. They are also, unfortunately, extremely good at absorbing heat and repelling moisture. These attributes put them near the top of the list of contributors to both the urban heat island effect and the combined sewage overflow problems that plague cities around the world. By laying a mantle of earth and vegetation on a rooftop, a building owner can mitigate, in a small but measurable way, these ills. A green roof absorbs rainfall, lowers rooftop temperature, and offers other benefits too. It extends roof life, earns points toward LEED (Leadership in Energy and Environmental Design) certification, creates wildlife habitat, and garners good publicity. And for many people, installing one is simply the right thing to do. These benefits will become even more important as temperatures and the volume of rainfall rise globally—as climate models predict they will.

The idea of insulating buildings with earth is not new. It has appeared in many incarnations around the world for thousands of years. What is new is the use of modern, lightweight materials to capture water and create conditions in which plants can thrive. Over the past several decades, European researchers have honed this technology, and Americans have brought the concept home. Chicago, Philadelphia, Seattle, and New York are among the cities actively using green roofs to help address water quality and infrastructure problems. Green Roofs for Healthy Cities, a North American industry association, reports that its members installed 4.3 million square feet of green roofs in 2010, twice the number of the year before.

The following pages explore the history of vegetated roofs, the structural engineering beneath them, and the plants best suited for them. Practical advice is included for readers who want to embark on their own projects. Also featured are profiles of an array of New York City green roofs, including a rooftop farm in Queens, a colorful retreat on a public housing development in the South Bronx, and BBG's own water-capturing rooftop meadow. Most of these roofs are high up and out of sight for all save a small number of city dwellers, but as more and more are built, their benefits will accrue and be felt by everyone.

The view from the living roof of Cook + Fox, an architecture firm in Manhattan, shows that a growing number of urbanites are greening their rooftops.

Green Roofs Past, Present, and Future

Linda S. Velazquez

Green roofs may be modern, but they're not exactly new. People have been covering their dwellings and other structures with layers of soil and vegetation since prehistoric times. Some of the earliest known earth-sheltered homes, constructed by Neolithic communities in Ireland and Scotland, were simple dwellings consisting of stone walls built into a hillside or mound so that the earth banked one or more walls and perhaps covered the roof as well. The well-preserved ruins of the Skara Brae settlement on the Orkney Islands in Scotland, which were probably inhabited until around 2500 BC, are a well-known example of this style.

Other cultures offer similar examples. In fact, different iterations of living roofs were widespread across the world, especially in cold climates, where they abounded for practical reasons: Earth-sheltered buildings were warm and cheap, and the material—essentially soil—was readily available. In Scandinavia, the idea took the form of pitched sod roofs built atop log houses. Turf was cut in sections from nearby fields and laid on a watertight layer of birch bark. The technique probably originated in prehistoric times and was common there through the 18th century. Norse settlers also brought the style to Ireland, the Faroe Islands, and other parts of northern Europe; later Scandinavian pioneers used it in Nova Scotia and the timber-scarce prairies of North America.

A related idea—the roof garden—also emerged in ancient times. In the Middle East, elaborate versions were constructed as embellishments on castles, estates, or religious structures. These were built not so much for their practical benefits as for the way they helped glorify an already impressive building.

The oldest surviving example is probably the Ziggurat of Nanna, a stepped, pyramidal tower of stone built around 2100 BC in present-day Iraq. Part of a large temple complex dedicated to the Sumerian moon god Nanna, the structure is thought to have evoked a bridge to the sky. Archaeologists believe that its terraces were planted with trees and shrubs.

Even more famous were the elaborate Hanging Gardens of Babylon, known as one of the Seven Wonders of the Ancient World. No archaeological evidence

A historic church in Hof, Iceland, features the type of pitched sod roof that was common throughout Scandinavia and other parts of northern Europe in centuries past.

or eyewitness accounts exist, but they were supposedly built by the Babylonian king Nebuchadrezzar II around 600 BC as a gift for his wife. The gardens were described by ancient Greek historians as a series of lush, vegetated terraces planted with flowering and aromatic trees, shrubs, and vines, selected and arranged to please the senses.

Luxurious rooftop terraces had many moments of glory throughout the centuries, including two well-known examples from the Italian Renaissance: the Palazzo Piccolomini of Pope Pius II and the Medici home at Careggi. Equally elaborate designs also flourished in the Aztec city of Tenochtitlan in Mexico at around the same time, and the Kremlin in 17th-century Russia contained a large, bi-level palace roof garden complete with fruit trees, vines, and a large pond.

Urban Oases

Vegetated roofs became valued as refreshing urban oases as the advance of the Industrial Revolution made cities increasingly crowded, hot, and dirty. In the late 1800s, lush rooftop gardens started sprouting up in London, Paris, Munich, and New York to provide respite for well-heeled city dwellers. In New York, the trend took off when Manhattan theaters, inspired by the popularity of outdoor summer theaters in the nearby suburbs, started staging musicals and concerts on rooftop decks.

The first such deck was built on Broadway's Casino Theater in 1882. Eight similar structures, including Stanford White's 1890 Madison Square Garden, soon followed. These popular summer venues usually included potted palm trees, ivy trellises, and sometimes even water features like pools and waterfalls.

By the 1920s, their popularity had waned as theater tastes changed, but they had inspired a related trend: rooftop restaurants on swank hotels like the Waldorf Astoria and the Hotel Astor. Here, New Yorkers dined al fresco all summer amid

What Is a Green Roof?

A green roof can be installed atop an underground garage or a 60-story skyscraper, and it may be called by other names, like *living roof*, *vegetated roof*, or *ecoroof*. What makes a roof "green," and what sets it apart from a mere roof garden or terrace, is what lies beneath the plants you see. Between that vegetation and the standard roof structure, every green roof is a carefully constructed sandwich of functional layers. These include a waterproofing layer, a root barrier, a drainage system, filter cloth, and a lightweight "engineered" growing medium in which the plants take root and grow. Both modular green roof systems, which arrive preplanted, and those that are layered in place on-site include these essential layers. When installed and performing properly, these layers work together to allow green roofs to perform the functions outlined on page 12.

The Skara Brae ruins in Scotland are well-preserved examples of the earliest known earth-sheltered homes; they were probably built around 5,000 years ago.

fountains, potted trees, and vine-covered pergolas. Beautifully planted penthouse terraces also emerged as a status symbol for the wealthy.

The 1930s saw the creation of two acclaimed urban roof gardens—the woodland, Tudor, and Moorish gardens of the Derry & Toms department store in London and the series of five extravagant neo-Renaissance roof gardens at Rockefeller Center in New York City. But these iconic examples marked the end of an era. The trend largely stalled with the Great Depression, and by the time the economy was ready to support such luxury building again, air conditioning was becoming widespread, reducing the impetus to create cool rooftop havens.

Modern Sustainability

In the 1970s, as the environmental movement got under way, the concept of using green roofs as a sustainable building technique took hold. In Germany, which was in the vanguard of green roof design, early examples of modern, lightweight vegetated roofs involved minimal plantings in a thin layer of soil on top of gravel rooftops. But scientists and builders were committed to improving the idea, and they made early advances in waterproofing, root-resistant barriers, drainage, soil science, and plant research.

German landscape architects Gerda Gollwitzer and Verner Wirsing published their influential book outlining the potential environmental benefits, *Roof Areas*

A vintage postcard shows the roof garden restaurant of the Ritz-Carlton Hotel in Manhattan as it appeared in 1918, when such decks were all the rage for theaters and restaurants.

Inhabited, Viable and Covered with Vegetation, in 1971. In 1975, the independent nonprofit organization Research Society for Landscape Development and Landscape Design (*Forschungsgesellschaft Landschaftsentwicklung Landschaftsbau,* FLL) formed, which helped crystalize the movement. The society remains a leader in the field, frequently updating the FLL Guidelines and providing European definitions, testing, and standards.

By the 1980s, better root barriers and other improvements had increased the lifespan of green roofs, which allowed greater acceptance in the European construction market. At the same time, the German government and municipalities began to encourage their installation with subsidies and ordinances. In 1996, Munich passed a statute requiring that newly built flat and slightly sloped roofs larger than 1,086 square feet be landscaped; Berlin passed a similar statute in 2000; and Stuttgart, Düsseldorf, Karlsruhe, and numerous other German cities soon followed.

Fourteen percent of German roofs are now green, according to one recent estimate, and that number continues to grow. Other European countries followed Germany's lead in the 1970s and '80s, including Austria, Switzerland, the Netherlands, France, Italy, the Scandinavian countries, and later the UK. Extensive, intensive, and hybrid versions are now widespread throughout Europe.

America's Turn

The United States has been much slower to embrace green roofs, but that's changing as the environmental and financial benefits become more apparent. With city governments leading the way with incentives and regulations to encourage their use, builders have been much more eager to include green roofs in both public and private projects.

Chicago has been North America's green roof leader for the past decade, thanks to several initiatives started by former mayor Richard M. Daley. After visiting Germany in 1998 and seeing its beautiful living roofs, he set out to make Chicago the model city for U.S. green roof construction. In 2000 the city completed a 20,000-square-foot, semi-intensive, retrofitted green roof on its city hall, a first among municipal buildings in the U.S. The project serves as a demonstration of how green roofs can improve rooftop temperatures and air quality and conserve energy. The roof surface is as much as 30°F cooler than surrounding roofs in the summer and saves thousands of dollars a year in utility costs. Chicago has also integrated sustainability programs throughout the city government and offers incentives and expedites permitting processes for greening initiatives. As a result, the city now has seven million square feet of green roofs built, planned, or under construction.

Municipalities and LEED

Other cities are following suit. In Portland, Oregon (where green roofs are called ecoroofs), their construction has been spurred by the need for better storm-water management. In 2008, Portland instituted its Grey to Green Initiative, with the goal of constructing 42 acres of new ecoroofs by 2013; the city set aside $6 million to fund incentives of $5 per square foot. Portland now has more than 300 ecoroofs and 130 roof gardens.

Similarly, Seattle has also initiated a series of incentives and regulations to encourage green roofs. Former mayor Greg Nickels supported their use for storm-water management and backed construction of green roofs on the Seattle Justice Center (completed in 2002) and Seattle City Hall (2003). The Big Apple has also recently jumped aboard. As part of Mayor Michael Bloomberg's PlaNYC, which lays out a strategy to meet several environmental challenges by 2030, New York City has been encouraging green building practices since 2008 with subsidies of up to $100,000 for green roof construction. New York also recently announced a plan to invest in green roofs, enhanced sidewalk tree beds, and porous sidewalks and parking lots as part of a strategy to reduce sewer overflow and clean up polluted waterways like the Gowanus Canal and Newtown Creek.

According to Green Roofs for Healthy Cities, a nonprofit industry association, there are government green roof regulations and investment in more than 20 state

Benefits of Green Roofs

By Beth Hanson

Add a bit of nature to a cityscape, and the benefits accumulate. A green roof helps a building's owner and residents, as well as the community at large. Here's how:

Storm-Water Management

Ordinary rooftops shed rainwater through storm drains into the sewer system. Many cities like New York have aged systems that mix this water with untreated sewage. When such sewers overflow, they flush raw waste into nearby waterways. Green roofs absorb a significant amount of the rainfall that hits them—as much as 70 to 90 percent in warm weather, 25 to 40 percent in winter—decreasing runoff and reducing the amount of debris and pollutants washed into lakes, streams, and rivers.

Energy Savings

Not only do green roofs improve energy efficiency by helping to insulate the building, they also reduce the workload for HVAC (heating, ventilation, and air conditioning) equipment. On a hot day, the surface of a black rooftop can get twice as hot as the ambient air. Rooftop HVAC equipment uses a lot of energy when it takes in super-heated air and cools it. A green roof reduces heat gain so that the HVAC system doesn't have to work as hard, which conserves energy. This also increases the lifespan of HVAC systems, saving replacement costs in the long run.

Longer Roof Life

Conventional roofs are exposed to sunlight and temperature extremes that degrade the roofing materials. A green roof shields the underlying layers, extending the lifespan of the roof—in some cases doubling it. Because a green roof is replaced less frequently, fewer roofing materials enter the waste stream.

Mitigation of Heat Island Effect

Conventional building materials absorb and retain heat from solar radiation during the day and release that heat at night. On a green roof, plants absorb solar energy and convert it to sugars. They also absorb and emit moisture. This means the roof doesn't heat up as much. An urban area with many green roofs will be cooler overall than an urban area with only conventional roofs.

Recources for Urban Wildlife

As development increasingly fragments wildlife habitats, green roofs can provide food and protection for birds and insects and act as "stepping-stones" for species that migrate through urban areas.

Amenity Space

Green roofs can add new outdoor green spaces for recreation in cities. Even inaccessible green roofs can provide a visual break from the grays and blacks of city streets and rooftops.

The green roof on Chicago City Hall, built in 2000, saves money in utility costs and has helped spur the green roof movement in the United States.

or city jurisdictions, including Virginia, Philadelphia, Pittsburg, Cincinnati, Milwaukee, and Washington, DC.

Other building industry organizations and certification programs are also helping to create standard practices and provide incentives. Of particular importance is the U.S. Green Building Council's Leadership in Energy and Environmental Design (LEED) program. Federal agencies and local and state governments are increasingly requiring new buildings to be LEED certified, and including a green roof is one way to earn points toward such certification.

Furthermore, as the green building market continues to grow, the costs of green roof construction will fall. Green roofs are destined to become ever more popular. The combination of favorable economics, innovative design and construction, and a growing awareness of the many environmental, aesthetic, psychological, and social advantages of green roofs and living architecture are simply too compelling to ignore.

Green Roof and Living Wall Trends

Linda S. Velazquez with Haven Kiers

Each year for our website, Greenroofs.com, we compile a list of the top trends in living roofs. We ask, What new ideas are sweeping our profession? Why do clients want a green roof? How are designers pushing the limits? These seven trends answer these questions in exciting ways and address a range of environmental and socioeconomic issues.

Green Roofs Plus Solar Panels

Combining green roofs and photovoltaic panels is a win-win situation. Photovoltaic panels work more efficiently at lower temperatures, so the cooling effect of the living portion of the roof allows the panels to be more productive. In return, the panels can also help shelter and protect the plants from the elements. Germany, in particular the Stuttgart region, is leading this trend, and other countries, including the U.S., are following suit.

Net-Zero Water Use

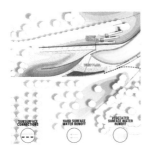

By harvesting rainwater and recycling wastewater for reuse, a building could theoretically be free from the municipal water grid. That's the ambitious idea behind Net Zero Water, a tenet of the Living Building Challenge, the most rigorous green building standards around. Since the initiative was developed in 2006, very few buildings have been certified, but many attempts are in progress. In pursuit of this goal, designers are integrating green roofs with other creative water-management techniques.

Green Affordable Housing

Healthy, efficient, and sustainable housing helps solve many environmental and social issues and doesn't have to cost more than standard affordable housing—it can actually cost less in the long term. Green roofs not only contribute to these overall goals but can also provide safe, clean, outdoor venues for relaxation and recreation in neighborhoods where they are too often lacking. The Brook in the Bronx (left; see also page 50) is one such example.

Green-Collar Job Training

Nonprofit groups as well as public-private collaborations are helping underserved youth and adults by offering training in the installation and maintenence of green roofs and walls. For example, the for-profit green company Green Living Technologies International has partnered with a Bronx high school to train students as certified installers. The students operate a profitable farmers' market and are being hired to install green walls and roofs across New York State.

Horticultural Therapy

Therapeutic green roofs enable hospital patients to enjoy the healing properties of nature. One such example: the 10,000-square-foot rooftop garden of the Schwab Rehabilitation Hospital in Chicago (right), designed to offer sensory therapy using plants and a 50-foot stream filled with koi. The garden also features areas where patients can relax or work on ambulation and wheelchair mobility.

Eco-Cities

Eco-cities and mega-developments, some recently completed, others in progress, use green roofs on a grand scale. For the Vancouver 2010 Winter Games, the Olympic Village (right) incorporated extensive and intensive green roofs on half of its buildings. In China, 350,000 residents will one day occupy the 12-square-mile Tianjin Eco-City, a showcase for new green technologies covered with green roofs and green bridges slated for completion in 2020.

Rooftop Farming

The growing number of city dwellers and the environmental costs of transporting food have inspired the concept of "vertical farms," multistory urban structures where crops grow indoors and on roofs. Many versions have been proposed, like Food City Dubai, a complex that would include stacked, hydroponically grown crops. On a smaller scale, existing rooftop farms prove the idea is a viable, even profitable, option in the here and now.

A Green Roof Glossary

Tracey Faireland

combined sewer overflow (CSO) Untreated water and sewage discharged into the environment from an overburdened combined sewer system. This type of system collects storm water and sanitary sewage in the same pipe. During a heavy rainfall, storm-water volumes can exceed the capacity of the system, causing it to overflow and discharge untreated sewage with the storm water into local bodies of water. Green roofs absorb rainwater and slow the travel time of runoff, thereby easing the burden on municipal storm-water systems during peak events.

drainage layer A green roof layer designed to direct the flow of excess water to roof drains. Some drainage-layer systems are designed to retain water so that plants can access it during dry periods. Typical components include gravel or similar material, perforated piping, and drainage sheets consisting of either special synthetic fabrics or a system of flow channels and storage chambers.

engineered soil A soil or growing medium that is designed to meet specific structural, planting, and drainage requirements and is a mix of both organic and inorganic materials. Green roof growing medium is one type of engineered soil. (See **growing medium.**)

evapotranspiration The combination of evaporation and transpiration (the release of moisture from within plant leaves). This natural process contributes to the cooling effect of green roofs.

extensive green roof A shallow green roof system with growing medium less than six inches deep and no permanent irrigation system. Such systems are usually designed to require little or no maintenance once established.

filter fabric A water-permeable synthetic fabric designed to keep fine particles from entering and clogging a drainage system. On a green roof, the filter fabric is installed between the drainage layer and the growing medium.

green façade A wall onto which rooted, climbing plants grow via a trellis or other framework attached to building's exterior.

gray water Wastewater collected from baths, showers, and sinks. Researchers are studying the viability of using gray water to irrigate landscapes and green roofs.

growing medium An engineered soil specially designed for specific uses (such as green roofs) and typically composed of coarse, lightweight mineral aggregates and a small percentage of organic material. (See **engineered soil.**)

hardscape Structures and other elements such as concrete pavers, benches, curbs, fountains, and walkways that are incorporated into a landscape or green roof.

heat island An area dominated by materials that build up solar heat and release that heat slowly after sunset. Structures typical of dense urban areas—asphalt and concrete parking lots and roads, dark-colored roofs, masonry buildings, and the like—contribute to the creation of heat islands. Surface temperatures of heat islands are hotter than ambient daytime air temperatures, and overall temperatures are warmer than surrounding rural areas.

impervious cover A surface made of material (such as concrete or asphalt) that does not allow water to pass through. Typical parking lots, sidewalks, roads, and roofs are examples of impervious cover.

intensive green roof A green roof system with a deep layer of growing medium (more than six inches) and a permanent irrigation apparatus that can support a variety of plants, including trees and shrubs. Such roofs are often designed as terraces or gardens and require continuous maintenance.

LEED (Leadership in Energy and Environmental Design) A building certification system developed by the U.S. Green Building Council. Buildings accumulate points toward LEED certification by employing design and construction strategies to improve human and environmental health. Depending on the number of points a project earns, it may receive certification at one of the following levels: Certified, Silver, Gold, or Platinum. Green roofs contribute credits if they achieve the following:
- maximize open space
- control the quantity and quality of storm water released by the building
- reduce the heat island effect
- are landscaped in a way that promotes efficient use of water
- optimize the project's energy performance
- are constructed using regional materials and/or rapidly renewable resources.

living wall An indoor or outdoor wall in which the growing medium, plantings, and irrigation system are integrated into the wall itself. A typical living wall might include modular panels containing plants and growing medium installed on vertical framework and attached to a wall.

Green Roof System

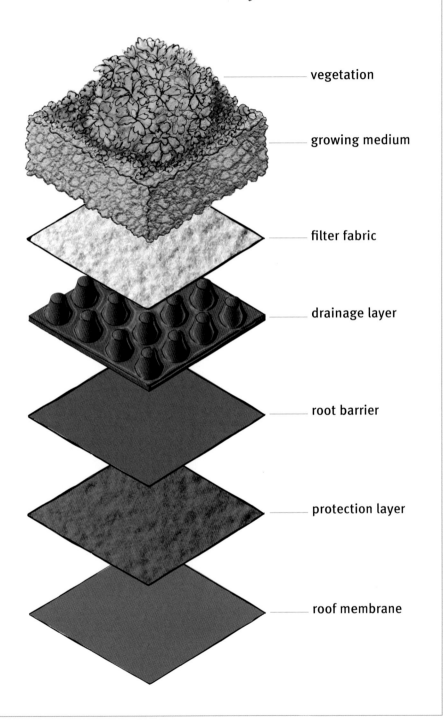

vegetation

growing medium

filter fabric

drainage layer

root barrier

protection layer

roof membrane

modular green roof system A system in which the plantings and growing medium are contained in trays or bags, which are installed on top of the roof membrane or protection layer.

permeability The ease with which water is able to move through a material.

pervious area An area that allows water to pass through it.

protection layer A synthetic fabric installed below the drainage layer to protect the roof membrane from damage.

rain garden A garden (also called an infiltration basin) designed to capture and absorb precipitation, especially storm-water runoff from roofs and hardscaping. Rain gardens are usually created in low-lying depressions and include water-loving plants, permeable engineered or natural soil, and often drainage piping and dry wells. They can be used in conjunction with green roofs to improve municipal storm-water management.

rainwater runoff Precipitation that is not absorbed or contained where it falls. (See **storm-water runoff**.)

roof membrane A flexible, waterproof layer that is adhered to the roof structure and is the primary waterproofing component of a roofing system. They are typically made of plastic, synthetic rubber, or asphalt.

root barrier A protective layer of dense, inorganic material such as plastic or synthetic rubber that is installed on top of the roof membrane to protect it from microbial activity and penetration by plant roots.

semi-intensive green roof A green roof system with a mid-range or mixed soil profile that has characteristics of both intensive and extensive green roofs.

storm-water management system A site-wide system designed to capture, contain, absorb, transport, and/or disperse precipitation that falls in a particular area. A green roof may be one component of a storm-water management system.

storm-water runoff Precipitation that is not absorbed or contained where it falls. (See **rainwater runoff**.)

urban heat island effect The higher average temperature of an urban area compared with the average temperature of surrounding rural areas. (See **heat island**.)

Transforming the Big Apple

Beth Hanson

When most people think of green space in New York City, they envision Central Park—that iconic green rectangle surrounded by a sea of gray concrete and black asphalt. But if New Yorkers were to look up while walking along the crowded sidewalks, they might catch a glimpse of some of the new green spaces growing above them. Green roofs are sprouting around the city in all kinds of surprising places—on top of office towers, schools, apartment buildings, public housing, and cultural institutions.

Or maybe it's not that surprising. After all, in many ways, New York is the perfect setting for a green roof boom. There are 22,000 acres of traditional tar and asphalt roofs that could use an update. They're dreadfully hot in the summer, and during storms, rainfall runs right off them, contributing to sewer overflow and flash floods. At the same time, most of these roofs are conveniently flat or nearly so, and in a city known for its astronomical real estate prices, laying some soil and vegetation on a roof may be the one way to disprove the age-old investment maxim, "Buy land. It's the only thing they're not making any more of."

Of course installing a green roof in New York City can be a special challenge. Soil, plants, and roofing materials, which already make a green roof more expensive than a simple roof replacement, have to be moved up bit by bit, one elevator load at a time or by crane. Labor is also more expensive here. Despite these downsides, a growing number of New Yorkers are going for it.

The green roofs featured on the following pages show both how challenging and how rewarding it can be to install them in New York City. Not one of the owners regrets the decision; they all say doing so was worth the cost and effort. Read on to find out how they managed to transform some of the city's tar beach into living, breathing, functional landscape that absorbs water, cools and purifies the air, and provides respite for birds, bugs, and people alike.

A sunflower grows in Queens—this one on the roof of a 90-year-old industrial building— among the many crops being grown by the rooftop farmers of Brooklyn Grange.

Connecting the Workplace to the Natural World

People are happier when they are connected to the natural world—that's the basic concept behind the theory of biophilia, and it's an idea that the architects at the Manhattan firm Cook + Fox are always emphasizing in their designs for clients. So when the firm moved into a new office, the partners decided to practice what they preach by installing a picturesque green roof just outside the windows to allow the whole staff to take in the view.

"A connection to nature is one of the themes of our work, and the view of our green roof from the studio has reinforced this," says Mark Rusitzky, a senior associate at the firm. Research has shown that work environments designed to provide such a connection are more productive and creative overall, an important benefit for a busy architectural firm. The roof also provides a ready example for clients interested in green building practices. This has become especially important since the firm has become known for designing the Bank of America Tower, which achieved LEED Platinum certification.

The office space was once the dining room of an upscale department store, and when Cook + Fox first relocated there, the expansive curved wall of windows over-looked a large, terrace-level roof that was closed off from the interior space by a row of offices. The architects removed those offices so that every workstation would have a view of the roof.

They wanted a green roof system that would be lightweight, low-maintenance, and affordable. It also needed to work with a nonrectilinear shape and be flexible

INSTALLED 2006   SIZE 3,600 square feet   TYPE Extensive
ARCHITECT Cook + Fox Architects
GREEN ROOF SYSTEM Green Paks by Green Roof Blocks, modular bag system
PLANT SUPPLIER Emory Knoll Farms and Jost Greenhouses
GROWING MEDIUM 4:1 shale/compost, from McEnroe Organic Farm
COST $10 per square foot
FUNDING Private, offset by NYSERDA grant
GOALS To provide an educational tool for clients, visitors, and employees

enough to be altered later if necessary. They chose a modular bag system, Green Paks, from the Missouri-based Green Roof Blocks, which not only conformed to the geometry of the roof, Rusitzky says, but was also the cheapest system available. Knitted polyethylene mesh bags (measuring 24 by 30 inches and 4 inches deep) arrived on-site filled with a growing medium containing 80 percent expanded shale and 20 percent compost.

A low-cost loan for the renovation and green roof installation, as well as funding from the New York State Energy Research and Development Authority (NYSERDA), a public corporation that funds research and incentives for alternative energy and energy efficiency, also helped keep the project affordable. Another key cost-saving measure was to use volunteer labor. "Our own employees helped install the roof, so that brought the cost down to about $10 per square foot," Rusitzky said.

On a baking hot Saturday in August, a team including 25 volunteers from the firm hauled hundreds of 55-pound bags up a freight elevator, out through an office window, and onto the roof. They laid the bags on top of a composite drainage layer–root barrier, cut a few slits in each bag, and added a slow-release fertilizer. Into each bag they planted six sedum seedlings from the 5,000 received from greenhouses in Maryland and Missouri.

"We installed and planted the whole roof system on a Saturday. Most architectural projects evolve over years, but this one provided instant gratification," Rusitzky says.

Project architect Mark Rusitzky, left, uses the Cook + Fox roof to educate and inspire clients. The system's plants grow in polyethylene bags containing growing medium; gravel channels provide storm-water control.

Once these windows overlooked a tar-paper roof; today, clients and staff alike enjoy the verdant view. As a bonus, summer temperatures on the roof have dropped by almost 40°F.

Over the next six weeks the architects watered the roof about twice a week, and the seedlings thrived. In the following months, wildlife appeared on the roof, including dragonflies, moths, gnats, flies, ladybugs, monarch butterflies, and even hawks.

All was idyllic until 2008, when the original, aged roof below the planting began to leak, and the entire roof had to be replaced. To get access, the firm had to move all the green roof packs, now flush with established plants, up one floor to an adjacent roof using a ladder conveyor system. When the roof repair was completed two months later, the roofer returned the packs to the original roof.

Happily, most plants survived the two moves remarkably well. Four years after its reinstallation, the roof looks as good as ever, and the firm reports that very little time is spent on maintenance. "We weed before we hold an event in the office and fertilize once a year," Rusitzky says.

Lessons Learned Double check—make that triple check—to ensure your underlying roof is in good shape before you install a vegetated one. The building's owner had originally told Cook + Fox that the roof was structurally sound, but, "as tenants, this was a risk we were forced to take, and unfortunately, the result was not the best-case scenario," says Rusitzky. "Moving the green roof to do the repair was a huge hassle."

Where the Wild Things Are

In a quaint mews in Brooklyn Heights, a carriage house holds a tiny grassland on its roof. Swaths of wildflowers and tall grasses mix with low-lying sedums. The view changes over the year as the perennials emerge, leaf out, bloom, and fade, and butterflies, birds, and bees arrive, feed, and depart. Spring's greens change to summer yellows, oranges, and blues, then to the ambers and mauves of fall.

Unlike most green roofs, overhead and out of sight, this one was designed to put on a show for its owners, who have the rare privilege of being able to look out the window and see their own green roof. (They live in the main house across the courtyard; the carriage house acts as their mother-in-law unit.) They wanted a meadow, so their green roof consultants, Amy Falder and Chris Brunner, partners in the firm Convert, decided to plant mostly native species of flowering perennials and grasses. This strategy involved a certain amount of improvisation, since using natives on green roofs is a fairly new approach. The installation also took place in fall, which limited the number of plants that were available for planting.

"We went to our supplier, who has mostly northeastern natives, in October and said, 'What do you have?' It made this roof more spontaneous and fun," says Falder. The pair left the nursery with grasses, butterfly milkweed (*Asclepias tuberosa*), yellow coneflower (*Echinacea paradoxa*), wild blue indigo (*Baptisia australis*), goldenrod (*Solidago sphacelata*), showy aster (*Eurybia spectabilis*), and more. They knew that planting a variety of different species would increase the chances that a critical mass would thrive. They also planted densely—about four plants per square foot—and used fairly mature plants, some of which had been growing in gallon pots all sum-

INSTALLED 2008   SIZE 800 square feet   TYPE Semi-intensive
LANDSCAPE DESIGNER Terrain NYC
GREEN ROOF CONSULTANT Convert
GREEN ROOF SYSTEM Layered on site
FUNDING Private
GOALS To create visual interest for the building's owners across the courtyard and a stopover spot for migrating butterflies

mer. "It was a little bit of an experiment. We were confident that some of the species would flourish, but we just weren't sure exactly which ones," says Falder.

Since the underlying roof is somewhat pitched, the construction of the green roof was unconventional. On top of the roof membrane, root barrier, and drainage mat, Falder and Brunner laid a geo-grid netting with banana-shaped slope-retention cleats attached, then threaded drip-irrigation lines throughout. The soil, an intensive blend, was bermed up to six inches deep in areas to provide more root space for the taller plants, its weight serving to hold the underlying roof elements down. They then spread a jute mat on top of the soil to keep it from slipping off and cut slits for the plants.

Four years later, the roof is flourishing. Though the 50 original goldenrod plants have dwindled to two, and the little bluestem (*Schizachyrium scoparium*) has almost disappeared, almost all the other plants are going strong. The New England blazing star (*Liatris scariosa* var. *novae-angliae*) has been prolific, and the bitter switchgrass (*Panicum amarum*), a beach grass native to the East Coast, has spread everywhere. "That's surprising because it's a big grass," says Brunner, "and it's growing even in the shallow soil."

The subsurface microdrip irrigation seeps water at root level and keeps the less drought-tolerant grasses and perennials going through dry spells. "The built-in irrigation is dialed down, and in the heat of summer, it's only on a few times a week," Brunner says. "But plants this size in only four inches of media need water in a

Chris Brunner of Convert visits the roof four years after it was planted and points out that the switchgrass has grown surprisingly tall in relatively shallow soil.

The roof's drainage system is protected by perforated boxes (left), which help minimize clogs. Pathways that allow maintenance access (right) were planted with low-lying sedums that can withstand occasional foot traffic.

dry spell." Convert applies a slow-release organic fertilizer once a year and makes monthly maintenance visits. "Because this roof is inherently natural and wild, we do minimal maintenance throughout the growing season, mostly managing the switchgrass," says Falder. "We try to keep it at bay because we don't want it to choke out the color palette." In the spring they remove the dead plant matter to lighten the roof load and reduce the risk of fire. The surviving species are doing so well that no one has even thought of trying to replace the ones that fizzled. "The roof is beautiful the way it is," says Falder "That's nature, that's succession, and the clients are happy. Why mess with a good thing?"

Lessons Learned It's best to design the green roof before any roof elements go down, says Brunner. "This green roof was designed after the waterproof membrane was already in place, so it wasn't really a cohesive design," he says. With a different membrane, the slope retention system might not have been necessary, for example, Brunner adds. "We've probably done 30 or 40 projects since this one, and this is still an issue. People decide they want to have a green roof and bring us in after they've already put that layer down or done a preliminary design. It's best to think of the waterproofing as integral to the system, not as an afterthought," Brunner advises.

A Green Roof Proving Ground

Although the utility giant Con Edison's business is selling energy, the company also works hard to encourage customers to conserve. To that end, the company has installed a quarter-acre extensive green roof on its facility in Long Island City, Queens, as well as half a million square feet of white roofing throughout New York City. Con Ed is monitoring the performance of both types of roof systems, in collaboration with researchers from Columbia University. The project is providing hard data in a field where numbers are still difficult to come by, and the results look surprisingly promising, especially when it comes to the green roof's role in managing storm water.

The green roof sits on top of Con Edison's training facility, the Learning Center (TLC), and it offers a spectacular view of the Queensborough Bridge and Roosevelt Island. It was a logical place to build a green roof, and in 2008, just as TLC's roof was scheduled for replacement, Con Ed's research and development department was thinking about investigating their potential. ConEd architect Chris O'Karma chose a modular green roof system using multicolored sedum trays arranged in blocks of red, green, and gold in an artistic, abstract pattern, and the company enlisted the aid of Stuart Gaffin, a researcher at Columbia's Center for Climate Systems Research who has been studying green infrastructure.

Gaffin's team placed equipment both below and above the roofing material to monitor temperature, heat flow, moisture, rainfall, and other key measurements. Since much of the data that exists on green roof performance doesn't differentiate among the various types of systems, Gaffin's team was interested in comparing ConEd's modular system with a nearby layered roof, as well as with ConEd's white roofs. Since data collection began in 2008, they have generated two white papers on the

INSTALLED 2008   SIZE 10,680 square feet   TYPE Extensive

OWNER Con Edison

GREEN ROOF SYSTEM modular, by GreenGrid

PLANT SUPPLIER Green Roof Plants, Emory Knoll Farms

COST $18 per square foot

FUNDING Private

GOALS To study the energy efficiency and water retention of a modular green roof

roofs' performance at both energy savings and storm-water management. In the first, the researchers compared the ConEd green roof with nearby black and white roofs. The green roof gained 84 percent less heat in summer than the black roof and lost 34 percent less heat in winter. (The white roof gained 67 percent less than the black in the summer and had little effect in the winter.)

When it comes to managing storm water, the green roof's performance was even more impressive. When the team crunched the numbers on the roof's water-retention capabilities for the second study, they found it able to absorb 30 percent of the rainwater that hits it annually—or an average of ten gallons per square foot per year. The layered system performed even better—retaining about half of the rainwater that hits it each year. That's more than 30 times greater than a recent New York City storm-water management report presumed that a typical green roof could.

The discrepancy, Gaffin says, is likely due to a scarcity of solid, well-sourced data in the field. "Often you'll see a number on something like water retention, and it's not clear whether it's for a single storm event or the average over a year, let alone how deep the soil layer is, or what type of vegetation was used. That's something I'm trying to change with my research," says Gaffin.

As a result of its low projection for water retention, the city's report had concluded that green roofs would be less cost effective at preventing storm-water runoff than other methods like cisterns and rooftop detention. Gaffin's numbers suggest otherwise. By his calculation, over the course of 40 years, a modular green roof can do

Columbia researchers used rain gauges and other equipment to track the roof's storm-water management performance and found it absorbed ten gallons per square foot per year.

A module's raised edge (left) allows for easy installation, and the plants eventually grow over and hide the edges. Sedums (right) retain impressive amounts of rainwater.

the job for two cents per gallon, making it the most cost-effective method of those considered. Gaffin also calculates that installing modular systems on New York's billion square feet of traditional rooftop space would prevent 10 to 15 billion gallons of storm-water overflow—or about halfway toward completely eliminating it.

"It's sad that green roofs were probably overlooked because of a bad number, but in the future, I hope contributions like mine will help city planners realize the great potential for green roofs as an affordable, practical approach to infrastructure problems," says Gaffin. "My dream is to gather even more data so that we can have real, solid comparisons for the key people making these decisions."

Lessons Learned Columbia University researchers are monitoring eight green roofs around New York City, all collaborations that began *after* the owner or representative had already selected a green roof system. "Now we're at a stage where we would prefer that the building owner let us choose the system and design the layouts for experimental purposes. If people want us to research their system, we now want more input in setting up the controls and variables," says Gaffin.

From Rooftop to Table

You can walk up to Brooklyn Grange, a one-acre farm conceived in 2009, but it's quicker to take the elevator. The farm is located on the rooftop of a seven-story industrial building in Long Island City, Queens, built in 1919. With the Manhattan skyline as its backdrop, Brooklyn Grange's farmers raise 60 different crops that yield about 14,000 pounds of produce a year, proving that with ingenuity, determination, and a lot of volunteer labor, rooftop farming in the middle of the Big Apple can be economically viable.

Behind the farm is a six-person partnership that includes a full-time farmer, an entrepreneur-turned-beekeeper, and four other friends with backgrounds in the restaurant business, food co-ops, and urban agriculture. The group formed in 2009 (and had originally planned for a site in Brooklyn, hence the name). After several months of intense fundraising, the group had cobbled together $200,000 from private equity, loans, grassroots events, and a Kickstarter.com campaign, which brought in $23,000. With that initial funding, the farm paid for the crane rental and permits needed to lift 1.2 million pounds of soil to the roof. An all-volunteer workforce helped the partners lay down the roof components, spread the soil, and get in their first crop, for an amazing $5 per square foot. Now, a $592,730 grant from the NYC Department of Environmental Protection is enabling Brooklyn Grange to open a second rooftop farm on a pier at the Brooklyn Navy Yard, which will double the group's arable land.

Despite its setting, Brooklyn Grange's challenges are pretty similar to those of a rural farm: finding the best methods to improve the soil, the most saleable mixture of crops, and the most efficient way to get the harvest to market. To maintain the

INSTALLED 2010   SIZE 40,000 square feet   TYPE Intensive

FOUNDERS Brooklyn Grange, a six-person partnership

GREEN ROOF SYSTEM Conservation Technologies

PLANT SUPPLIER Seeds from Johnny's Select and Fedco

GROWING MEDIUM Rooflite from Skyland: 50 percent expanded shale, 50 percent compost

COST $5 per square foot ($200,000 total)

FUNDING Private equity, loans, grassroots fundraising, Kickstarter.com

GOALS To raise agricultural crops and offer educational opportunities

fertility of its Rooflite soil blend, the farmers fertilize with a fish emulsion foliar spray, ProGro organic fertilizer, potash, and compost. "We collect compost through the Western Queens Compost Initiative," says partner Gwen Schantz. "We add sawdust from a woodworker in Greenpoint and mashed-up oyster shells for calcium. Over the winter, we improve the soil by planting a cover crop of vetch and rye clover."

Because Brooklyn Grange is committed to accepting vegetable waste from the general public to help keep compostables out of the waste stream, the farm is not eligible for organic certification, Schantz says. "But we use organic practices," she adds, "and participate in the Northeast Organic Farming Association," a nonprofit that promotes organic growing methods.

In its second season, the farm fine-tuned its crop mix, adding more greens and flowers for cutting and planting fewer cabbages and broccoli than in the first year. "The direction we're heading now is toward planting an increasingly smaller number of varieties," says Schantz. "We'll always have at least 50 to 60 different crops, though, and always try new things." Best sellers in both seasons were tomatoes and greens. "They're huge and will remain a large part of the planting," she says. "And carrots, peas, and peppers help maintain the diversity and are really essential."

To get their harvest to market, the farmers load up a minivan and drive the produce to customers in Manhattan, Brooklyn, and Queens. "Half goes to restaurants—there are about ten that are steady customers—and half goes to our farmers' market stand

Ben Flanner, Chase Emmons, and Gwen Schantz are members of the six-person partnership that founded and operates Brooklyn Grange.

The farm yields 14,000 pounds of produce per year using organic practices. Of the 50 or 60 different crops grown, tomatoes and greens have been the best sellers.

and members of our CSA," says Schantz. During its first year, Brooklyn Grange had to hustle to get clients. "Now people are coming to us," she adds.

After two years of rooftop farming, "our big conclusion is that this works," Schantz says. Urban farming increases green space, generates economic activity and jobs, and helps New Yorkers connect more closely to nature. "It's such a win-win— our business is growing, and we're going to see more rooftop farms popping up as other people follow our lead. In the meantime, we'll continue growing and building more farms."

Lessons Learned A guerilla green roof installation like Brooklyn Grange's first farm is simpler and cheaper than the new roof at the Navy Yard, says Schantz. To maintain the warranty of the new million-dollar roof at the Navy Yard, the Grange has had to work with specific contractors and use specific products. "Everything has to be aboveboard and is incredibly expensive—three times the cost of the first roof," she says. "Working within the confines of a government grant has been an amazing lesson in how complicated and time consuming this can be."

A Green Roof with a Twist

What's the best way to update an iconic space where art, music, street life, and academia converge? For Lincoln Center, the answer was an architectural redesign that included an accessible green roof. Called the Illumination Lawn, the center's new roof is perfect for barefoot lounging, picnicking, and listening to concerts and performances. It's shaped like a twisted rectangle, or hyperbolic paraboloid, and it sits above a glass-sided restaurant and film center. Two of its corners rise up and two dip down, one to ground level, creating a stepped entryway for visitors to climb up, take in the view of the Henry Moore sculpture and reflecting pool below, and enjoy Lincoln Center from a new perspective.

The lawn was one item on a major renovation agenda for Lincoln Center, says Heidi Blau, an architect with the firm FXFowle, which collaborated on the project with Diller Scofidio + Renfro. Among the mandates for the north plaza, where the lawn is sited, was improving the connection between Lincoln Center proper and its neighbor, the Juilliard School, by removing a bridge across 65th Street and bringing campus life down to street level.

"There wasn't a stitch of greenery anywhere on the bridge plaza, but it was the only outdoor space for Juilliard students. One of our goals was to create a welcoming new space where they could hang out," says Blau. Lincoln Center also wanted to block out street noise, since the north plaza is sometimes used as a performance space. The roof's highest side was placed along the street to shield the plaza from the city's hustle and bustle, says Blau.

In addition to all of these contextual challenges, the designers of this green roof faced three special hurdles. First, they needed to accommodate the weight of the soil,

INSTALLED 2010　　SIZE 7,200 square feet　　TYPE Intensive
OWNER Lincoln Center
ARCHITECT Diller Scofidio + Renfro in collaboration with FXFowle Architects
TURF CONSULTANT Frank Rossi, Cornell University
GREEN ROOF SYSTEM American Hydrotech
FUNDING Lincoln Center redevelopment funds, New York State, federal government
GOALS To create green space for the public and mitigate street noise

grass, and as many as 300 visitors at a time. Second, they had to find a way to prevent the soil and grass from sliding off the significantly pitched roof. Third, they needed a grass blend that would be able to withstand heavy foot traffic and look green and inviting most of the year.

To support the roof's live and dead loads, the team devised a six-inch concrete slab on a metal deck structure, with beefed-up columns and beams below. A honeycomb-shaped retaining structure was stretched over the roof to contain the soil layer, which varies from 8 to 12 inches deep because of the roof's shape.

"We needed some kind of retention system, at least for the first year, to allow the grass to really sink its roots down and prevent the soil from sliding off," says Blau. For the lawn, the project team brought in Cornell University turf expert Frank Rossi, who recommended a mix of 90 percent tall fescue (*Schedonorus phoenix*) and 10 percent Kentucky bluegrass (*Poa pratensis*), which was added for its teal hue.

"It will look good even into November—and it's fairly durable for foot traffic," says Blau. A built-in irrigation system includes pop-up sprinkler heads that provide regular watering, and the grass is periodically fertilized, overseeded, and mown. A system of drains and check dams below the surface keeps the moisture level consistent throughout the slope. The result is an irresistible emerald green lawn with a shape and location like no other that has become an extraordinarily popular attraction for the campus. "Once the spring comes, there are people on it all day long, well into the evening," says Blau.

The lawn sits on top of a glass building that houses a restaurant and film center and offers a new perspective of the adjacent Henry Moore sculpture and reflecting pool.

The roof dips to a stepped entry point (left) that allows the public to climb up. The team consulted a turf expert, who recommended a mix of tall fescue and Kentucky bluegrass for durability and color (right).

It may not be the maintenance-free green roof that many purists aspire to, but it's brought the concept to a level that most New Yorkers can relate to—one where they can climb up and plunge their toes into green.

Lessons Learned No matter how carefully you plan ahead, a green roof will always be a work-in-progress, so always be prepared to make adjustments. The Lincoln Center team went so far as to create a quarter-scale model of the roof in a Jersey City parking lot and tested the system through a couple of growing seasons.

"We had not seen a lot of lawns this shape," Blau says, "and we wanted to make sure it really worked." Still, no one anticipated how popular it would be, which has resulted in a tremendous amount of wear and tear on the grass at the roof's entrance. As a result, the team periodically alters the path people use. "This is a problem, but it's a good problem. People want to come and experience the lawn," says Blau.

Teaching Sustainable Skills

It's late spring at Alfred E. Smith Career and Technical High School in the Bronx, and a talkative and energetic group of students is up on the school's green roof explaining its latest project—an experiment tracking how solar panels placed above the vegetation will be cooler and thus perform better. As they describe their findings and take visitors on a tour of the modular system and planters on the school's 2,000-square-foot atrium roof, the students' enthusiasm is palpable. After all, many of them actually helped create the green roof from scratch. Drafting students surveyed the site before installation, plumbing students built the roof's rainwater harvesting system, and carpentry students built the wooden planters for the vegetables. Some students even gave a presentation on the roof at a conference on green roofs in New York City schools.

The project seems tailor-made to provide hands-on experience for a vocational high school, but its existence is largely due to a chance encounter. In 2007, the school science club, led by speech teacher Nate Wight, took a field trip to the offices of Sustainable South Bronx (SSBx). There Wight learned that SSBx had access to funding for a school green roof and was looking for a school and teacher to partner with. SSBx director Miquela Craytor asked him if he was interested. "Definitely, definitely, definitely," was his answer.

Wight realized that the school's open-air, walled atrium would actually make an ideal site for a green roof. The split-level area is a half-story above ground and sits atop an automotive shop class and boiler room. Over the next several years, he navigated the permitting system at the NYC Department of Education and

INSTALLED 2010   SIZE 1,600 square feet   TYPE Extensive
OWNER New York City Department of Education
GREEN ROOF SYSTEM Modular
PLANT SUPPLIER Prides Corner Farms
COST $45,000
FUNDING Grants from the City Gardens Club of New York City and the NYC Department of Environmental Conservation
GOALS To help students connect with nature and learn green-collar job skills

School Construction Authority. In 2010, the school installed the modular green roof system—the first approved green roof on a New York City public school.

The completed roof will be a focal point for the curriculum of Bronx Design and Construction Academy, the new vocational high school located in the building. The new school, founded by Wight and some of his fellow teachers in 2011, is specifically focused on teaching building trades—electrical, HVAC (heating, ventilation, and air conditioning), plumbing, and architectural drafting—with a special emphasis on green-collar job skills. Graduates receive an endorsed diploma, which will speed their admission to a building trades union, a welcome benefit for students in one of the poorest congressional districts in the country. Experience working with a modern green roof gives them an additional boost, and the faculty has incorporated it into several aspects of the curricula.

"They'll have real-world, hands-on experience that will help solve environmental problems," says Wight, who now teaches ecology. "That's going to put them ahead of a lot of other people, whether they go directly into the workforce or to college."

At the same time, the roof will help give their work a scientific context as well as a better understanding of how they can contribute to a more sustainable world. They'll continue to run experiments like the one investigating solar panels and rooftop vegetation and use the roof to study ecology. Recently, for example, Wight assigned his ninth graders to write a memoir of a plant or animal on the green roof using ecological concepts such as succession.

Students have been involved in all aspects of building and maintaining the roof. They designed and built the planters, water the plants, and harvest the produce grown here.

The roof was built with a vocational curriculum in mind, but it also allows students to conduct investigations in ecology and other natural sciences.

"Most adolescents today, especially those in the city, are disconnected from nature. Our students in particular don't have much access to parks and nature," Wight says. "Spending a full period out on the green roof surveying the plants and animals—looking at the spider webs, the sedum, the flies, and worms—they can see it all in action and really connect with it."

Lessons Learned The way to a teenager's brain is through his stomach. "I notice the students' connection to the edible plants growing in the planter-box beds is much stronger," says Wight. "They also have more opportunities to get their hands dirty by working on and maintaining the annual crops in the planter boxes. If I were to do this again, weight load permitting, I'd add more planter boxes for edible plants. I love the sedum—it has great environmental benefits—but an edible garden is so much more interactive."

A Little Bit Country

David Puchkoff wanted it all: an apartment in New York City with the setting of a country house—complete with a screen door and a porch swing with a view. By installing a 1,200-square-foot green roof on his West Village building, Puchkoff got that and more. From a sixth-story aerie, he and his family now have sweeping views of Manhattan, a sedum "lawn" that he weeds while watching birds and butterflies, and an added layer of insulation for their living space below.

Puchkoff, a real estate developer, was something of a green roof pioneer. When he moved into his building in 1975, he had rights to develop the roof area. "But I never felt comfortable just putting up decking and potted plants. I wanted something else but was not sure just what," he says. In the late 1980s, Puchkoff first heard about green roofs being used in northern Europe. "I loved the idea, but I didn't know how to install it all on an existing roof, what kind of plants to use, and how much soil to lay down."

The idea stayed dormant until 2002. That year, he visited a friend's lakeside cottage, where a porch overlooking a garden and lake provided inspiration for the type of space he wanted on his roof. Around the same time, the Earth Pledge Foundation held a seminar on green roofs, which he attended to get details on how to put his plan into action.

Puchkoff then hired an architect friend to design a rooftop folly, an enclosed galley kitchen with a rustic attached porch. Then he set about creating the green roof, a process that included vacuuming 2,400 pounds of growing medium up to the roof through a five-inch tube. Puchkoff, his daughter, and two laborers planted the roof's 2,200 sedum plants. "I decided not to use contractors, because I understood the con-

INSTALLED 2005   **SIZE** 1,200 square feet   **TYPE** Extensive

OWNER David Puchkoff

GREEN ROOF SYSTEM American Hydrotech

PLANT SUPPLIER Emory Knoll Farms

COST $12 per square foot

FUNDING Private

GOALS To create a private recreational space and increase the insulating properties of the roof

cept and could buy the materials myself," he says. The installation was labor intensive and took about a week, but it didn't require extensive professional expertise.

Since then, Puchkoff has added a small herb garden and bulbs in containers along the porch, and a dwarf Japanese maple (*Acer palmatum*) grows in a boat-shaped planter. But the most striking feature of the roof is the juxtaposition of the rustic porch and urban skyline. It all adds up to a charming venue for many family activities. "I have coffee and read the paper there in the morning, then we have lunch up there, and we eat dinner on the roof every night from the end of May to the end of September."

Removing unwanted volunteer plants is the main maintenance chore on this roof. "At least once a week I put a couple of hours into weeding," says Puchkoff. The vegetation has waxed and waned, and the planting was partially destroyed in 2011 when workers replaced 22 deteriorated lintels on one side of the building. Almost half the succulents were killed, but Puchkoff points out that these were once-in-a-lifetime repairs. "Most of the work that goes into a building like this would have a minimal effect on the roof," he says. The plants have since been replaced, and the roof garden is on the rebound.

As a real estate developer, Puchkoff has weighed the costs and benefits of green roofs from a professional perspective. He installed a 3,000-square-foot green roof on another building he owned several years ago and says the tenant who rented the adjoining space was excited about it. It was definitely a plus, but a green roof is

Puchkoff has had great success with container plants like the lilies (*Lilium orientale*) along the porch (left). The succulent "lawn" (right), planted with the help of his teenage daughter, is also thriving and includes many sedums as well as hens and chicks (*Sempervivum* species).

The enclosed kitchen and porch, inspired by a friend's lakeside cottage, provides owner David Puchkoff and his family with a charming venue for enjoying their green roof.

still a hard sell to business partners, since the payback period isn't easy to predict, he says. "It adds insulation and stops heat buildup, but because so many factors go into a building's costs, it's impossible to calculate the savings precisely. It's so building specific."

Building owners look for clear payback periods, usually within three to five years, so investing in a green roof requires a shift in thinking. "I would guess you're going to get a return on your investment in ten years, but not much sooner," says Puchkoff. Still, the technology and resources have evolved to the point where a green roof often makes good business sense. "The savings are longer term, but they're there," he says.

Lessons Learned Installing a green roof without the help of a contractor or consultant was possible in 2005, when Puchkoff put in his. Today, it's even easier now that more sustainable-construction businesses and resources exist. Many companies sell individual green roof components, including plans, lining and barrier materials, growing media, containers, and plants. Nonprofit greening organizations can also lend support. "Someone with intelligence and resources can do some research and put the pieces together themselves using not very skilled labor," says Puchkoff. Doing so can save 25 to 30 percent of the project's cost, he estimates.

The Bronx Is Blooming

Mott Haven, a predominantly Puerto Rican neighborhood in the South Bronx, contains one of the highest concentrations of housing projects in New York City. More than half of its residents live below the poverty line and receive some kind of public assistance. But amid the tenements, projects, and industrial buildings of Mott Haven and the nearby neighborhoods of Melrose and Morrisania, low-income green building is booming, and sleek new apartment buildings are providing area residents with housing options that promise clean air, lower utility bills—and quiet green spaces like the Brook's 4,000-square-foot green roof.

The new 189-unit Brook is one of 16 residential structures owned and operated by Common Ground, a public-private partnership that provides housing for low-income workers, people with HIV/AIDS, and chronically homeless people. On-site services are available to help tenants deal with health issues and find education and employment. For Common Ground, the benefits of green building are twofold. "Not only are we creating a better environment for our tenants, we're also creating a more efficient, cost-effective model," says Common Ground spokesperson Lyle Churchill.

These same benefits are also spurring construction of nearby buildings like the brand-new Via Verde, which features stepped and connected rooftop gardens where residents can grow fruits and vegetables; Forest House, which boasts a 10,000-square-foot hydroponic farm on its roof; and El Jardin de Selene, a new building in the Melrose Commons development with solar panels and three green roofs.

The Brook's green roof is a simple, open space surrounded by a high fence and gravel perimeter, bisected by a wide, brick-red path dotted with fixed benches. "Residents use the space as a spot to hang out with their families and guests or practice

INSTALLED 2009   SIZE 4,000 square feet   TYPE Extensive

OWNER Common Ground

LANDSCAPE DESIGNER Hanna Packer, Town and Garden

GREEN ROOF SYSTEM Layered on-site

GROWING MEDIUM SkyGarden extensive green roof media

FUNDING Common Ground

GOALS To contribute to an overall green building strategy and provide outdoor green space for residents, guests, and staff

early-morning yoga, and staff members eat lunch or read the newspaper there," says building director Paul Pavon.

The roof's planting is a colorful low-lying carpet of reds, greens, yellows, and blues woven from eight species of *Sedum*, and native, magenta-flowered fameflower (*Phemeranthus teretifolius*), with chives (*Allium schoenoprasum*) interspersed throughout to add a wild, natural look to the otherwise manicured design. "The chives also have fantastic blooms in the spring," says garden designer Hanna Packer of Town and Gardens, the New York firm that executed the project.

The building's architect originally envisioned a more elaborate semi-intensive design, with berms of deeper growing medium incorporated to allow multiple levels of plantings, but that would have been more costly than the budget allowed. So instead, Packer came up with an innovative way to create the a similar effect using a more affordable extensive system. Her design mimics the contours of a topographic map. After spreading four-inch layer of soil, she and her team laid a jute mat on top to hold the starter plugs in place until they were established.

They watered the roof during the plants' establishment, but since then, nature has done the watering, Packer says. A year and a half later, the planting has evolved into a paisley-like pattern, rather blurred as some species have migrated a bit—but that was part of her plan. "It's always fun to see what happens to a design after a few years," she says.

Gravel borders keep paths clear and protect plants from scorching and possibly catching fire by growing too near rooftop heating and cooling structures (left). The original paisley pattern of the planting has blurred (right), but that was part of the designer's plan.

To keep costs down, the team decided to forgo berms and instead created a textured effect by using different-colored sedums accented with tufts of chives.

Packer says she hopes the roof functions as a tranquil escape from the concrete jungle. "Spending time there calms you down and puts your mood up," she says. This is especially welcome to tenants of the Brook, many of whom contend with extraordinary stresses. "But it doesn't matter if a green roof is on a high-income or low-income building. Everybody benefits," Packer adds.

Lessons Learned The Brook's green roof is among 17 that Packer has designed, and she has learned that having the right materials is crucial. "Work with trusted suppliers, and check your sources very carefully. On another job, I worked with a green roof soil supplier whose media was not up to spec and contained too much rock." To ensure that the mix was perfect for projects like the Brook roof, Packer visited the blending facility at SkyGarden before she decided to work with them. "Now I know that every batch is going to be blended to the same standard."

A Green Roof Laboratory

On the roof of the New York City Department of Parks and Recreation's sprawling Five Borough Administration Building on Randall's Island, there are plants everywhere—in pots and planters, overhead and underfoot. There are also composting bins, beehives for fostering pollination, and monitoring equipment that's collecting data on weather and roof conditions, some of which is streaming live on the department's website. The lush, colorful rooftop, complete with picnic tables, looks a little bit like a park itself, but it's actually a real-world laboratory where the Parks Department is investigating potential green roofs for its buildings and gathering years' worth of performance data to share with the public.

"We need to spread the word," says John Robilotti, senior project manager and the man behind this ambitious collection of systems. Today, Robilotti, a civil engineer who has worked for many years on capital projects for the Parks Department, is one of the most passionate green roof advocates around, but he's a relatively recent convert, who was nudged into the project by the department because of his engineering expertise and experience in landscape architecture. Not long after installing the building's first section of vegetated roof—a modest, 800-square-foot layered system—Robilotti became hooked on the idea. "When I saw firsthand the benefits it provided for a pretty low cost and small amount of effort, I realized a green roof should be a no-brainer for any roof replacement."

He was pleased with this early success, but he wasn't satisfied. He wanted to find out how the model could be tweaked. Could he get similar results with shallower soil? Could modules do the same job more cheaply? How much water and soil would he need to grow native wildflowers? To find the answers to his questions, Robilotti

INSTALLED 2007–2011   SIZE 29,000 square feet   TYPE Intensive, extensive
OWNER New York City Department of Parks and Recreation
GREEN ROOF SYSTEM Multiple
COST $200,000 (labor and maintenance provided by Parks Department employees)
FUNDING New York City Department of Parks and Recreation, public and private grants, donations from green roof suppliers
GOALS To serve as a testing site for various green roof systems and educate the public about the benefits of green roofs

built a series of test plots on the roof, each with a different set of variables. Over the course of four years, he researched, planned, designed, and installed the 25 different systems that now cover almost 30,000 square feet of the facility.

"I like to gloat that we have the most diverse green roof in the world," Robilotti said. "It's the only place where you can view so many different systems side by side." Each one was installed by Parks Department employees and volunteers, and they include modular and layered systems, green walls, hydroponic vegetable towers, systems using native and nonnative plants, and plots for testing different soil mixtures. "The three basic variables in our systems here are the composition of the growing medium, the depth of the growing medium, and the types of plants," says Robilotti. "Each system has some different combination of these."

A tour of the building's roof winds around HVAC equipment and other structures, with each turn revealing a new type of planting: There's a 20- by 40-foot raised bed filled with native perennials, a colorful red and green checkerboard of sedums and pavers, a sea of metal trays fabricated in the building below and filled with sedums. Fifteen hydroponic vegetable towers sit next to a 4,000-square-foot vegetable garden. Peeking over one ledge you see a lawn planted with tall fescue (*Schedonorus phoenix*) and *Vinca* species in the atrium below. Peer over another ledge and you see a lower roof lined with large plastic cisterns where rainwater is collected for irrigation. Homemade wooden planters overflow with sedums used to take cuttings for propagating. *Wisteria* species and trumpet vine (*Campsis radicans*) climb the legs

The roof is strong enough to support planters full of wisteria and trumpet vine climbing up trellises, as well as picnic tables where staff members can take their lunch break.

For this modular vegetated wall system, the plants were established in a horizontal position in a greenhouse, then mounted on the wall once the roots had taken hold.

of a trellis, and planters topping the parapet walls trail sweet potato vines (*Ipomoea batatas*) and junipers (*Juniperus* species).

Real-time data on the roof's temperature, humidity, barometric pressure, rainfall, and storm-water runoff is streaming on the Parks Department's website, and Robilotti's team is compiling historical stats from each system for publication online so that scientists, green roof professionals, and the public will be able to compare green roof options. "We started this to educate ourselves, but it's turned into an opportunity to educate New Yorkers, school groups, and municipalities here and abroad," says Robilotti.

Already, as a result of the work done at Five Borough, the Parks Department has installed ten 1,000-square-foot green roofs on recreation centers around the city, many of which are accessible to the public. These roofs are also the sites of a study the Parks Department is doing in conjunction with Columbia University to investigate the suitability of native species for green roofs (see "Going Native?," page 90).

After 33 years at the Parks Department, Robilotti plans to retire in 2012. He will leave behind a rooftop covered in plants and an unparalleled array of green roof systems that he hopes will inspire other New Yorkers to transform some of the acres of traditional tar roofs. "I've seen what was once a dead space slowly transformed into a living ecosystem that attracts birds and bees, cools the air, saves energy, and helps keep the local rivers clean. The potential for using them to improve the city—the world, actually—is huge."

Clockwise from top left: Robilotti discusses the pros and cons of using native perennials; purple coneflowers thrive on the roof; plastic pots and pregrown trays used for demonstrations; wildflowers grown from a widely available seed mix in a raised planter; testing a mulch mat made of coconut fiber; and various sedums in soil-depth trials.

Lessons Learned: Field Notes from Above

In his four years of researching, planning, designing, and monitoring 25 different roof systems, John Robilotti has learned a few things. For instance:

- Sedum can survive in as little as a single inch of soil, but the deeper the growing medium, the more biomass the plants will gain. Up to a point, that is. "This effect maxes out at six inches. Beyond that, you're just adding weight to your roof and not getting much more benefit," says Robilotti.

- By the same token, there are diminishing returns for adding soil depth when growing tall perennial plants. "They need a minimum of six inches," according to Robilotti, "but there's not much point in giving them more than a foot."

- Added insulation is just the beginning. "Everyone thinks that green roofs save energy because they're good insulators, and they are. But they save even more energy by cooling the air that gets sucked into the HVAC equipment," he says. Robilotti has used an infrared gun to check rooftop temperatures. On 90°F days, the black sections of the roof get up to 170°F, while the vegetated sections remain about 90°F. "Imagine how much harder it is for the AC to cool down the air coming from a 170°F roof."

- Experimenting with new plants is worth the effort. Robilotti is collecting detailed data on carefully selected native plants, but he's also willing to improvise. "For one plot, I just tried a commercial mix of northeastern wildflower seeds, and they did incredibly well and for a minimal cost."

- The DIY approach can save a bundle. "We do everything on a shoestring, so for every system we have, we went straight to suppliers for growing media, for plants, for modules, and we ended up paying a fraction of what we would have if we'd used a green roof company," says Robilotti.

- There's no such thing as the "best" green roof. "People ask about that all the time, but there's no single answer," says Robilotti. "It depends on so many things—the condition of the existing roof, the budget, the owner's goals, and the amount of maintenance the owner is willing or able to do."

- The environmental benefits are free. "Look at it this way, even using a conservative estimate, green roofs pay for themselves by extending the roof life to 50 years or more," says Robilotti. "Even if you don't give a hoot about clean water or the urban heat island effect, it's worth doing. Everything else—the energy conservation, the storm-water management, the climate impact—come without having to pay an extra cent."

Added Value

Pull up one of the Adirondack-style lounge chairs on the Solaire's terrace-level green roof and enjoy the million-dollar view. The sweep of riverfront before you includes the New Jersey shoreline, New York Harbor, the Statue of Liberty, and river traffic in the Hudson just below. And the terrace itself—a lush, colorful garden—is as lovely as it is environmentally functional.

A second green roof on the top floor further supports the building's ambitious goals for sustainability. With both rents and occupancy rates higher than those of most conventional high-rises, the Solaire is proving that going green not only saves energy and money over the long term, it also attracts a growing number of tenants who want to pursue a sustainable lifestyle.

The Solaire's two green roofs are classic examples of intensive and extensive designs. The 4,800-square-foot intensive green roof system on the 19th-floor terrace is a communal space open to all residents. Its irrigated soil layer, which ranges from 6 to 18 inches deep, supports trees, shrubs, and herbaceous perennials. It's also designed to absorb 70 percent of the rainwater that reaches it and to channel the rest to a 10,000-gallon basement cistern, where it is filtered and used to irrigate the roof and a ground-level park.

The 5,000-square-foot extensive system above the 27th floor is a much simpler affair—a sedum lawn in four inches of soil. Its purpose is entirely environmentally functional. Together the two systems cover 75 percent of the building's roof area, meeting the stringent green building requirements for all structures within the borders of the neighborhood's state-run development authority.

INSTALLED 2003   SIZE 9,400 square feet   TYPES Intensive, extensive
OWNER Albanese Development Corporation
LANDSCAPE DESIGNER Balmori Associates
GREEN ROOF SYSTEM American Hydrotech
COST Intensive roof: $50 to $60 per square foot; extensive roof: $25 per square foot
FUNDING Private, with $2.7 million tax credit from New York State
GOALS To comply with Battery Park City's green guidelines and provide outdoor recreational space.

Battery Park City now includes 26 residential towers. Three of them, including the Solaire, have LEED Platinum certification, and the neighborhood's sustainability features are gaining cachet. When the building opened in 2003, 10 percent of its tenants were drawn to it because of its sustainability, says Michael Gubbins, vice president of residential management at Albanese Development Corporation. Today 60 percent of renters say that's why they chose to live here.

"Even in a slow market we have full occupancy, and in a strong market we get a 10 percent premium on rents because we're in an environmentally friendly building," says Gubbins.

The 19th-floor roof is popular with residents, Gubbins says. The landscape design firm Balmori Associates created a space with four quadrants—garden "rooms" set apart by hedges of trees, tall shrubs, and planting beds. Growing in the beds are grasses, flowering plants, and groundcovers in compact groupings that create clusters of color, including species and cultivars of *Rosa, Spiraea, Rudbeckia, Begonia, Pachysandra,* and *Sedum.* The plantings create a parklike setting for residents who come out to relax in lounge chairs or picnic.

Tenants never see the building's highest rooftop, where a sedum bed skirts satellite dishes and the base of a mechanical room clad with photovoltaic panels. The sedum planting is thriving, but not in its original form: "We started with maybe 15 varieties, and half of them have disappeared," says Mark Thomann, director at Balmori. "Even

The Solaire's uppermost roof (left) combines a simple extensive green roof system with solar panels. The terrace-level roof (right) is an intensive system that is designed to support trees and shrubs like river birches and roses.

Mature plantings on the communal terrace help divide the space into distinct areas, provide shade, and contribute to the parklike atmosphere.

though we researched this sedum mix, we found that the pigeons like certain species, particularly the red ones. They eat the entire plant."

Thomann and his colleagues at Balmori hope that success stories like the Solaire will fuel a bigger trend toward including green roofs in newly built residential real estate projects. "Developers need to understand the payback, and have it driven home," says Thomann. The Solaire and nearby new luxury green high-rises are showing the way.

Lessons Learned Originally, bamboo was planted by the landscape designers to create a screen between the four terrace garden quadrants. But despite its reputation for being extremely hardy and fast growing, in the end, the bamboo was too fragile for this setting. "We planted the roof in August, and because of the heat and intense wind, the bamboo got windburn," says Thomann. Eventually, it was replaced with river birch (*Betula nigra*) and serviceberry trees (*Amelanchier* species), two native species that are thriving in the harsh conditions 19 floors up.

"In all landscape projects, you learn as you go which plants adapt and thrive in any given conditions. Since then, we've been researching the viability of using more localized native plantings," says Thomann.

Saving Energy in a Cost-Cutting Era

The U.S. Postal Service's boom years were in the last century, before the dawning of email, Facebook, and Twitter, but as part of its greener facilities strategy, the agency has made some 21st-century updates to one of its largest distribution centers. A 2½-acre green roof and other energy-saving technologies recently retrofitted onto the Morgan Distribution Center in New York City are cutting edge—and together are saving the agency a million dollars a year.

The Morgan Center, a landmarked building constructed in 1933, occupies an entire block on the west side of midtown Manhattan. Inside, its 3,000 employees sort as many as 12 million pieces of mail each day. Its semi-intensive green roof was the brainchild of engineer Shalini Mohan, whose firm URS was hired to oversee an energy overhaul of the facility. In addition to replacing 1,600 windows and installing new energy-monitoring equipment, USPS needed to replace the aged, leaking roof. "I was fully aware that they were trying to get greener and greener," says Mohan. "So I approached them and said, 'Can I take a look at doing something fun with the roof project?'"

A green roof was not only fun; it also made good business sense, Mohan asserted. It would reduce the building's energy costs and increase the lifespan of the roof to 50 years—twice as long as that of the previous roof. And since the roof had originally been built to hold heavy mail-sorting machinery, it required no structural upgrades, which would keep costs down. Its highly visible location was also a nice public-relations bonus in light of the USPS's desire to highlight its new agency-wide goal of cutting energy use by 30 percent by 2015. It was not a hard sell. "Our only mandates were to keep the cost under $5 million and to save energy," Mohan says.

INSTALLED 2009   SIZE 109,000 square feet   TYPE Semi-intensive

OWNER United States Postal Service

LANDSCAPE DESIGNER Elizabeth Kennedy Landscape Architects

ENGINEER URS Corporation

GREEN ROOF SYSTEM Tecta America; layered on-site

COST $41 per square foot ($4.5 million total)

FUNDING USPS

GOALS To demonstrate USPS sustainability initiative as it gains heating and cooling savings, recreational space for employees, and storm-water containment

During construction, builders replaced the 10 percent of the roof that was damaged and then installed the green roof layers. Next came the complicated task of transporting 2,000 cubic yards of engineered soil up to the rooftop. Crews used special industrial vacuum equipment set in reverse to blow the soil seven stories up from a holding pen at street level. Over three weeks, a crew planted thousands of sedums, grasses, and herbaceous native perennials, as well as nine serviceberry trees (*Amelanchier* species) along the path that bisects the roof.

Two years after completion, the open, airy space looks and feels like a patch of prairie transplanted from a few thousand miles to the west. The golden grasses flutter in the breeze, and the late-summer colors include the muted pinks and yellows of cinquefoils (*Potentilla* species), yarrow (*Achillea millefolium*), and sedums. Though only a stone's throw from the Empire State Building, it's still quiet enough to hear the hum of hundreds of bees and the occasional chirp of a cricket.

But the rooftop isn't merely bucolic scenery. It has contributed to a 52 percent drop in energy use since the upgrades, which have saved the building $1 million in the first year. The roof probably accounts for a very small portion of that—the original calculations predicted $30,000 a year in savings due to its insulating properties. Still, certain signs suggest that it is saving even more energy than expected. For example, heat gain on the roof has been reduced to the point that the air handlers on the floor below have hardly been in operation, says Mohan.

The underlying roof structure is strong enough to support containers with serviceberry trees. The trees are hanging in there, despite taking a beating from the wind and saltwater spray.

The roof provides a peaceful respite in the middle of Manhattan (left). Vegetation includes sedums, grasses, and native perennials (right), which attract bees and other insects.

In addition, a Columbia University research group tracked rainfall on the roof for June 2011 and found that it prevented 77 percent of the water from entering the New York City sewer system, said Wade McGillis, lead researcher. During peak downpours, which have the greatest impact on combined sewer overflow, the roof reduced storm-water flow by as much as 97 percent. The researchers also found that the roof mitigated acid rain, raising the pH from 4 to more than 8 once it had passed through the plants and soil.

No matter how you look at it, the roof has been a real boon for the agency. Not only has it helped to improve the sagging public image of the USPS, it has demonstrated that real benefits can come from institutional efforts to go green—and Facebook and Twitter notwithstanding, that the USPS has the ability to adapt and innovate in the century ahead.

Lessons Learned Two blocks in and seven floors up from the Hudson River, the wind can be intense. "We didn't anticipate that it would be as nasty as it is up there on the roof," said Mohan. The wind whips saltwater spray in off the Hudson, and the serviceberries planted on the roof haven't handled those conditions very well, she reports. "In hindsight, I wish we had used shrubs instead of trees or had chosen a different species of tree. This is one of those things that you can't figure out until you've actually experienced it."

Caring for the Natural World

When you walk through Regis High School, a Jesuit school on Manhattan's Upper East Side, the stately hallways crowded with clean-cut boys in uniforms make you feel as if you've traveled several decades back in time—until you reach the sixth-floor rooftop. There you see a 20,000-square-foot planting of sedums, herbs, and native perennials, a large solar panel array that supplies 5 percent of the school's power, a weather station, astronomical observatory, and several beehives. The system will help reduce the school's annual energy costs and provide students with an innovative new science classroom. The whole project dovetails with the Jesuit community's mission to connect with God by caring for the natural world.

The idea of installing a green roof first came up in 2006, when Regis conducted an energy audit. "It made me realize how much we were wasting in terms of energy, cost, and usage in our building and in society in general—how much we waste all the time," says Regis president Father Philip Judge.

High on the list of things to be improved was the school's cracked and blistered 100-year-old roof, which had lost its insulating ability and was in need of full replacement after years of being patched and layered over. Around the same time, the Society of Jesus published an ecology decree urging all members of the Jesuit order to renew their commitment to environmental stewardship as part of their spiritual mission. "So in a sense, installing a green roof seemed like a great opportunity to restore our relationship with the world around us," says Judge.

Father Judge and Brian Peterson, Regis's science club leader, attended a green roof design course organized by Green Roofs for Healthy Cities, a nonprofit industry association. There they met Amy Norquist, CEO of Greensulate, a green roof design

INSTALLED 2010   SIZE 22,000 square feet   TYPE Intensive and extensive
OWNER Regis High School
LANDSCAPE DESIGNER Greensulate
FUNDING SOURCES School endowment, grant from the Hyde and Watson Foundation for demonstration green roofs
PRIMARY PURPOSE To engage the school community in environmental change, reduce energy costs, and create a new community and educational space for the school

and consulting company, and started to put their plan in action. In 2010 Regis had Greensulate install a green roof on the high school building.

The completed project is surprisingly spacious and sits on an open rectangle that surrounds the school's internal courtyard. Tall parapet walls and bulkheads divide the space into distinct sections, and a planked walkway runs around the perimeter, taking you around corners, up and down stairs and through archways, with different garden "rooms" revealed at each turn. A variety of intensive and extensive plantings includes stretches of low-lying sedums and berms holding tall grasses; pink, purple, and blue phlox (*Phox* species); and alliums (*Allium* species), sage (*Salvia* species), lavender (*Lavandula* species), and other herbs.

"We have a brand-new space we can start using for the science department and the environmental club, and we'll be able to expose our students to new possibilities and new technologies," says Peterson. "At the same time, we're all becoming more conscious of the impact of climate change and environmental degradation." Regis has also partnered with Columbia University researchers, who installed monitoring equipment on the roof to supply data for their own green roof studies. They are collecting data on pH levels, turbidity, and dissolved oxygen of water from different parts of the roof, including two nonvegetated sections, to determine whether the water running off the green roof is healthier. Regis students are working with them, collecting water samples from three sections of the roof.

The roof includes both intensive and extensive sections. The berms of deeper growing medium are able to support tall grasses (left), while a variety of *Sedum* cultivars flourish in the shallower, extensive areas (right).

A planked walkway winds around the perimeter of the roof. To the left are berms of deeper soil that support grasses and herbs. To the right is the shallower, extensive section.

Jesuits have a long history of environmental awareness, says Judge, but they have recently become more directly focused on sustainability. The order's leadership has asked all its schools and churches to make their buildings energy efficient and is helping the farmers they work with globally to develop more sustainable practices. They are also launching programs at Jesuit universities to promote theological reflection and scientific research on the environment, says Peterson. "This is very exciting. Our leadership is giving us a mandate for the very thing we're doing."

Lessons Learned Peterson and Judge spent several years researching green roofs before jumping in. "Learn as much as you can on your own before engaging a green roof company," says Peterson. "Ours was an evolving process because we had a lot of time to think it through. But I think the most important lesson is to actually do it."

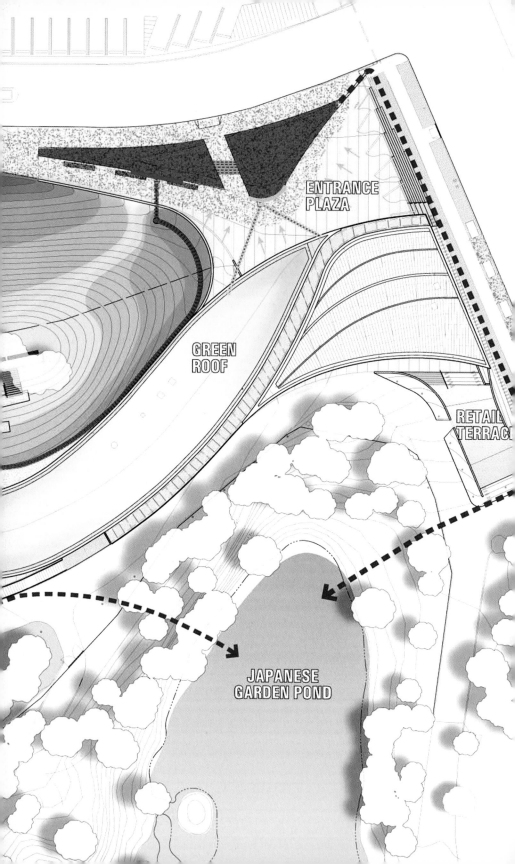

ENTRANCE
PLAZA

GREEN
ROOF

RETAIL
TERRAC

JAPANESE
GARDEN POND

A Water-Wise Welcome

Since first opening its gates to the public a century ago, Brooklyn Botanic Garden (BBG) has filled its 52 acres with beautiful, expertly curated plant collections and educated countless visitors about the benefits of gardening and urban greening. So it's fitting that the Garden has entered its second century with a project that accomplishes both of these missions in a strikingly modern way. The 9,400-square-foot living roof of its new Visitor Center adds 40,000 specimens to its collection and demonstrates the substantial environmental benefits of integrating a green roof with functional rain gardens. The interlinked system will conserve hundreds of gallons of water each year and capture all the storm-water that falls onto the building and entrance plaza, easing the burden on the city's overworked sewage system and helping to keep local waterways clean.

The question of how to deal with storm water was a challenge from the start, says Aaron Booher of the landscape architecture firm HM White, which designed and managed the project. "Originally, it was going to be channeled to underground storage tanks and then released slowly into the sewer system. But we recognized this as a real opportunity to showcase a new type of garden feature," he says. The result is a daisy-chain system in which one component fills up and channels water to the next. Water works its way through the chain, with the plants and soil soaking it up along the way.

The green roof is the largest surface area to capture water. Rain percolates through its plants and down into the growing medium and the layer of water-retention fabric below. If a storm dumps more precipitation than the roof can hold, excess water is directed through a gutter system to three sunken rain gardens containing water-

INSTALLED 2012   SIZE 9,400 square feet   TYPE Semi-intensive
OWNER Brooklyn Botanic Garden
ARCHITECT Weiss/Manfredi
LANDSCAPE DESIGNERS HM White and Convert
GREEN ROOF SYSTEM Layered on-site
FUNDING Public and private contributors, including the City of New York
GOALS To contribute to storm-water retention and educate the public

loving plants like switchgrass (*Panicum virgatum*), thread-leaf bluestar (*Amsonia hubrichtii*) and black gum trees (*Nyssa sylvatica*). Any water that isn't taken up by the rain garden plants or nearby soils flows into a duct that leads to the nearby Japanese Hill-and-Pond Garden. Subsurface drip irrigation with capillary fabric has been built into the green roof system for times of drought; however, once the plants are established, the roof should be largely self-sustaining.

Unlike most urban green roofs, many stories up and out of plain sight, BBG's is visible and meant to be looked at. From some angles, the roof's serpentine shape and the plants' contrasting swaths of color make a bold visual statement; from other perspectives, it seems to recede into the surrounding landscape. "It looks like a rippling hillside that blends into the berm beside it," Booher says.

Since the roof is part of a public garden, Booher knew it had to be more exciting horticulturally than a basic sedum-covered roof. He and the rest of the design team wanted a versatile display that would demonstrate seasonality and maintain a strong winter structure. BBG also wanted to include a variety of regionally native plants. "We knew a meadow-type ecosystem would achieve this," Booher says. The team researched options and then tested potential cultivars and species on-site for a full growing season in specially designed flats.

The roof is planted in large swaths of spring bulbs like snowdrops (*Galanthus nivalis*) and petticoat daffodils (*Narcissus bulbocodium*); flowering perennials like

BBG's Visitor Center was built against a berm set with walkways and an overlook, allowing the green roof to be seen from several vantage points (left). Visitors can view the roof as it changes seasonally; snowdrops (right) are among the first spring bulbs to bloom each year.

The living roof is integrated into the surrounding landscape, which includes newly planted rain gardens and BBG's historic flowering cherry collection.

purple prairie clover (*Dalea purpurea*) and butterfly milkweed (*Asclepias tuberosa*); and cool- and warm-season grasses, all of which create an ever-changing seasonal display. In late winter, the previous year's growth is trimmed back to make way for the spring-flowering bulbs. In the summer, the grasses dominate, their palette changing from chartreuse and pink to orange, purple, and magenta, and then to gold in the fall. Over the winter the color fades, but the structure remains. The plantings are intended to draw hummingbirds, butterflies, and lots of bees throughout the year.

With nearly one million people visiting the Garden each year, the Visitor Center roof is a show that will have a constant audience, most of whom will probably be getting their first up-close view of a functioning green roof. "It's an exciting opportunity to educate so many people about what a green roof can do," says Booher.

Lessons Learned For an intensive landscape construction project like this, make sure the landscape contractor is on board early in the process, especially if you're committed to using less typical plants, which may need to be custom-grown from seed at a nursery in order to be available in sufficient quantities at the right time. "The plants we're featuring are not so widely available, so we had to do some scrambling. Remember, the window of opportunity for acquiring the plants is really critical," says Booher.

The Nuts and Bolts of Green Roof Construction

Yessica Mariñez

Proper design, installation, and maintenance are essential to ensure that a green roof performs its environmental, economic, and aesthetic functions. Here are the nuts and bolts—and dirt and roots—of how a roof goes green.

Structural Considerations

New Buildings Building a green roof on a new building is much easier than retrofitting one to an existing roof, because a new roof deck can be designed specifically to support the weight of the green roof's plants, soil, water, irrigation system, and protective layers. In turn, adding a green roof may affect how some other systems in a new building are designed. The added insulation from a green roof reduces heating and cooling requirements and may allow smaller HVAC equipment to be used, for example. Piping and fixtures for watering the green roof plants can also be incorporated into a new building's plumbing design, and the roof's overall drainage system could include drainage for the green roof.

Retrofits Building owners and their project teams must consider specific physical issues before designing a green roof for an existing building. One critical task is to determine how much weight the roof deck—the roof's underlying structure of beams, columns, and joists—can support. Roof decks are typically made either of wood or steel-reinforced concrete, which can bear greater loads. The engineering team must also assess the condition of the roof deck. Leaks, for example, can cause wood to rot, metal to corrode, and concrete to crack and flake, all of which affect load-bearing capacity. Retrofits may require reinforcing the roof's structural elements or repiping some of the plumbing. (See "The Feasibility Study," page 81, for more details.)

Pitch and Layout Flat rooftops, the most common roof style in large cities, are on the whole more suitable for green roofs than pitched roofs. Pitched roofs may require a system of stops, buttresses, structural steel supports, and anchors to hold the green roof elements in place and to distribute the gravitational load evenly, which

Green roofs are specially constructed with multiple layers that support the vegetation and growing medium and protect the underlying roof components.

may require special maintenance. According to two leading international green roof organizations, Green Roofs for Healthy Cities, in North America and the FLL (German Landscape Research, Development, and Construction Society), in Germany, a green roof should not be installed on a roof with a slope greater than 40 degrees. In addition, a sloped roof limits design possibilities and generally rules out recreational use. Other factors to consider include the roof's size and layout and the location of exhaust pipes, bulkheads, or water towers.

Design and Intended Use

If you plan to include seating or play areas, make sure the deck can handle the added loads of people, furniture, planters, and other amenities. The design must also include safety features, walkways, and maintenance access to mechanical equipment, parapets, and drains. Buildings are also subject to specific codes regarding issues like fire safety, maximum loads, insurance, and tax abatements, all of which may affect the design.

As a rule of thumb, green roof growing media (soil) weighs approximately seven pounds per square foot, per inch deep, when fully saturated. Plants add to that weight: Low groundcovers (widely used in extensive systems) add one to two pounds per square foot; herbaceous perennials and other larger plants add considerably more, roughly three to five pounds per square foot.

An **extensive system** (with soil cover approximately two to six inches deep) typically weighs 10 to 45 pounds per square foot and places a relatively small load on the roof, making it the best choice for roofs with a wood-based roof structure. Such roofs are common among prewar, walk-up buildings in New York City, where extensive systems cost approximately $20 to $25 per square foot to install. Typically, plants grown on extensive green roofs are limited to drought-tolerant groundcovers like sedums.

Intensive systems are deeper (up to two feet of growing media) and heavier (45 to 200 pounds per square foot) than extensive green roofs and are often designed to support a wide variety of vegetation, including herbaceous perennials and sometimes also shrubs and trees. To support extra soil and heavier plants, intensive green roofs require a roof structure with a high load-bearing capacity. The plants themselves, which also usually need irrigation, may need to be placed over load-bearing walls or columns. At $30 or more per square foot, intensive systems are more expensive to install than extensive systems.

The Green Roof System

Part of what makes a green roof green is the system of layers put in place beneath the visible planting surface. These layers give green roofs a high insulating value, help manage water, and extend the lifespan of the underlying roof.

The soil layer of an extensive system is shallow and relatively lightweight. Such systems will support drought-tolerant groundcovers like sedums with very little supplemental irrigation.

The roof's **waterproofing membrane,** the first layer installed, keeps water from seeping into the building. Although not technically part of the green roof itself, it is an essential safeguard. Among the different types are liquid-applied membranes, which create a seamless surface; layered systems made of felt and asphalt; and EPDM (ethylene propylene diene monomer), a synthetic rubber placed in overlapping layers. There are also inverted roof membrane assembly (IRMA) systems, in which the insulation lies on top of the waterproofing membrane, the reverse of a typical roofing system.

A **protection barrier** (sometimes called a root barrier) lies loosely on top of the waterproofing membrane. It cushions the roof and prevents the plants' roots from indenting or penetrating the membrane. This barrier is typically made of sheets of polypropylene, PVC (polyvinyl chloride), or thermoplastic polyolefin (TPO).

A **drainage mat** sits on the protective barrier and contains small reservoirs that hold excess water when the soil and vegetation are saturated. During dry spells, the water in these reservoirs is drawn back into the growing medium and helps keep plants hydrated. The drainage mat also protects the waterproofing membrane.

Filter fabric is a tightly woven mesh that allows excess water to drain from the soil and provides the first line of defense against potentially roof-invading roots. This layer also keeps large soil particles and debris from clogging the roof's drainage system.

The **growing medium, or soil layer,** anchors the plants, sustains their growth, and retains moisture. For weight and drainage considerations, green roofs require specially engineered mixes containing mostly lightweight inorganic matter such as perlite and expanded shale and clay, along with a smaller proportion of organic materials with a high capacity to hold water like peat moss and decomposed wood bark, mixed with nutrient-rich content such as humus.

Vegetation is what gives a green roof its "green" (and many other colors). Extensive systems are usually planted with low-maintenance groundcovers that are drought and wind tolerant. For intensive systems, there are hundreds of species to choose from, depending on soil depth, climate, and goals. (See "Green Roof Horticulture," page 84.)

System Types

There are two main ways to install a green roof. In a **modular system,** commonly used in extensive green roofs, the plants are started in soil-filled trays (typically one by two feet and made of recycled plastic) at an off-site nursery. When the plants reach maturity, the trays are delivered, and the installer lays them side by side on top of the root barrier. The plants eventually grow about an inch over the height of the trays, forming a seamless layer of vegetation. One advantage of modular systems is that individual trays can be temporarily removed to access the roofing membrane.

Filter fabric helps protect the underlying layers from root damage and allows excess water to seep into small resevoirs in the drainage mat below.

The Feasibility Study

Before construction can begin, an engineer must conduct a feasibility study to determine whether the building can support a green roof and, if so, which type of system will work best. The engineer first visually inspects the overall condition of the roof surface. He or she may conduct probes to get a better view of the underlying structure. On concrete roof decks, the engineer may take core samples and have their compressive strength tested. Steel beam sections may also be lab-tested for tensile strength. The engineer then calculates the dead and live load capacities.

The dead load is the weight from the roofing system itself, including the green roof. Live loads are temporary and may include people, equipment, furniture, planters, or snow. The total load capacity determines the type of system the roof can support. In general, concrete decks are more likely to support intensive systems. Some wooden decks that cannot support even an extensive system can be reinforced to do so.

The engineer or architect also inspects the roof as a whole. The location of mechanical equipment could impact the green roof layout. Parapet height is also a factor: For example, New York buildings must have a parapet wall or railing at least 42 inches above the roofing surface; a green roof raises the surface, so a railing system may need to be added to extend the height. Any necessary upgrade or maintenance should be handled before the green roof is installed.

Another advantage is the instant gratification of seeing a flourishing greenscape take shape over the course of a day (rather than months).

In a **built-up system,** the installer lays the soil directly onto the filter fabric and plants on-site. Depending on the planting method (seeds, bulbs, transplants, plugs), these can take a year or longer to become established. If bulkheads or mechanical equipment break the roof into sections, the installer constructs those sections separately. **Vegetated mats,** which are unrolled like sod onto the growing medium, are a variation on this method that provides an immediate green cover.

The Project Team

Like any construction project, a green roof installation requires the coordination of many players. The client (typically the building owner) determines the overall scope of the project with the aid of all or some of the following professionals:

A **green roof consultant** advises the client on the advantages and disadvantages of the different green roof systems for the building, helps select system components and vendors, and may help assemble the rest of the team.

An **engineer or architect** conducts a feasibility study (see above) to evaluate whether a green roof is workable for the building. As part of the study, a **structural engineer** determines the existing roof's load capacity. The engineer/architect also designs and oversees necessary repair work and ensures that the design integrates with the existing roof system and maintains its integrity.

A **green roof manufacturer** designs and develops the green roof system itself. Some manufacturers are generalists, but others specialize in particular types of green roofs, so before choosing a provider, determine your system. A **roofing manufacturer** advises on the selection of the waterproofing membrane and other components.

A **horticulturist** comes up with a list of suitable plants based on system, climate, and landscaping goals. He or she may also work with a **plant nursery** and/or a **landscape architect,** who designs the layout and style of the green roof, especially if it has recreational use.

The **roofing contractor** performs the roofing repair or replacement in anticipation of the green roof installation and may either install the green roof or subcontract a **green roof installer** to construct the green roof system. The contractor coordinates scheduling, mobilization, and materials delivery to the site.

An **expeditor** obtains the work permits and documentation from the municipal buildings department and other agencies to make sure the green roof complies with building codes. Department of transportation approval may also be needed to close streets or sidewalks when materials are hoisted to the roof, often by crane, which also needs a permit.

On smaller projects or ones with a limited budget, the engineer/architect or the green roof installer may also serve as the green roof consultant and deal directly with the green roof manufacturer.

Warranties

Many roofing manufacturers offer an NDL (no dollar limit) warranty on their systems, ensuring that the owner will be reimbursed for the full cost of replacing the roof—covering materials *and* installation—for the entire term of the warranty, typically 15 or 20 years. Because a properly installed green roof can increase the life of the roofing membrane, some roofing manufacturers will extend their warranties by 5 to 10 years when a green roof is paired with their system.

The NDL applies to the roofing system as a whole: A green roof is part of the warranty's "overburden," which includes any structure installed on top of the roof, such as a recreational deck. To make sure the green roof installation does not void an existing warranty, the roofing manufacturer should be consulted for approval, and the installation must follow the manufacturer's specifications. Green roof installers also offer warranties, though for a much shorter period (usually five years), combined with maintenance plans. An installer's warranty typically covers against improper installation

Tray modules are installed side by side on top of the root barrier. One advantage of this type of system is that trays can be easily removed later to access the underlying roof.

that damages the green roof elements. In addition, the nursery may offer a warranty to cover plants that die prematurely.

Maintenance

Green roofs, like all roofs, will deteriorate if they are not kept in optimal condition. To prevent damage, the entire roofing system—including the waterproofing membrane, parapets, bulkheads, flashing, and copings—must be well maintained. In addition, a green roof typically involves a professional maintenance plan, in which a contractor regularly waters, weeds, fertilizes, trims and edges, tests soil nutrient levels, clears drains, removes debris, and inspects the irrigation system.

The contractor also oversees plant health (avoiding pesticides and strong fertilizers, which could contaminate runoff water) and keeps walkways and parapet walls clear of weeds and overgrowth. Typically, green roof installers provide maintenance plans for one to five years, including up to a dozen annual visits for the first two years and two to three yearly after that. Intensive systems may require more frequent visits. Twice-monthly inspections from spring to fall (year-round in warmer climates) should include weeding, replacing displaced soil, clearing drains, and removing debris. The maintenance plan should follow the recommendations of both the roofing manufacturer and the green roof manufacturer so as not to void any warranties.

Green Roof Horticulture
Edmund C. Snodgrass

There are thousands of plant species that will grow on a green roof, from the ubiquitous easy-care sedums to higher-maintenance cacti and meadow grasses to challenging but impressive trees and shrubs. Choosing the right ones requires thought and care. Here are the factors to consider.

Plants for Different Types of Living Roofs

The primary determing factor is the type of system on your roof: extensive, intensive, or semi-intensive. The main distinctions are soil depth and access to irrigation, which will greatly affect the types of plants that will thrive.

Plants for Extensive Systems These are the least expensive, lightest systems. They contain only two to six inches of growing medium and may not have an irrigation system, so plant choices are limited to those that thrive in shallow, low-nutrient soils. Drought-tolerant, perennial groundcover species and cultivars of sedums (stonecrop), houseleek, fameflower, hen and chickens, and ice plant (*Sedum*; *Sempervivum*; *Phemeranthus,* syn. *Talinum*; *Jovibarba*, and *Delosperma*) are your best bet. These plants readily store water in their leaves, are shallow rooted, tolerate gravelly media well, and don't require much fertility or irrigation.

Because of the huge number of *Sedum* species—there are hundreds—and because of their affordability and adaptability, sedums have emerged as the top choice for extensive roofs. Sedums are also good for any roof for which the primary purpose is functional. If you want to save on cooling costs, slow the flow of storm water, or extend the roof's life, sedums and other low-maintenance groundcovers will give you a return your investment in a reasonable period of time.

There are *Sedum* species and cultivars for nearly every roof condition—shade, full sun, drought, average moisture, etc. This variety also provides a rainbow of foliage and flowers, allowing you to create changing patterns and textures throughout the seasons. You may decide on a design that calls for a single species that looks almost like turf, one that incorporates different-colored sedums planted in drifts, or one in which several species are interplanted for a quiltlike effect.

Versatile, hardy sedums have emerged as the top choice for extensive roofs. They are affordable, drought tolerant, and come in a rainbow of colors.

Plants for Intensive Systems If your roof has adequate load-bearing capacity, you can consider an intensive system with plants that require more frequent watering and deeper, heavier soil (6 to 12 inches or more) with a higher organic content. You can also approach this choice from the other direction: Decide which plants you would like—trees, shrubs, vegetables, or grasses—then build or reinforce to accommodate them. An intensive system is also best for recreation and will allow for a more traditional garden with plants that can withstand foot traffic. There are more horticultural options for an intensive roof, but they will cost more and require more maintenance.

As you would for a ground-level garden, choose plants for their color, texture, height, bloom time, and year-round interest, but remember to select those that are as wind- and drought-tolerant as possible. Short to midsize grasses (*Bouteloua, Carex, Festuca,* and *Sesleria* species) are good choices, as are flowering plants and herbs such as yarrows, alliums, bellflowers, pinks, oreganos, phlox, cinquefoils, self-heals, and violets (*Achillea, Allium, Campanula, Dianthus, Origanum, Phlox, Potentilla, Prunella,* and *Viola*). Some species of cacti—prickly-pear (*Opuntia humifusa*), for example—work well, especially as accent plants. Small bulbs like crocuses, daffodils, grape hyacinths, and tulips (*Crocus, Narcissus, Muscari,* and *Tulipa*) add color and texture in spring. Consider accenting with tough, easy-to-grow annuals such as zinnia, cosmos, cornflower, and marigold (*Zinnia, Cosmos, Centaurea,* and *Tagetes*) cultivars. Trees and shrubs require yet more soil, water, and maintenance and consequently more load-bearing capacity

The deeper soils of intensive and semi-intensive systems support a wide variety of plants, including cacti like prickly-pear (left), grasses, and small bulbs like daffodils (right).

Choosing Plants for Your Living Roof

Before heading for the nursery, consider these factors:

Purpose Is the planting primarily functional—intended for, say, storm-water containment or heat reduction? Or is its purpose aesthetic—to soften a severe urban landscape or provide an attractive spot for entertaining?

Engineering Constraints How much additional weight can your roof bear? How is the pitch and drainage? Your engineer's findings will determine the type of green roof systems possible and the depth of soil your roof can accommodate.

Accessibility Is the roof readily accessible and does it have a nearby water source? If the answer to both questions is yes, you may be able to grow a wide range of plants on your roof.

Expected Interaction Will people walk over or spend time on the green roof on a regular basis? If so, include paths and unplanted areas in the design, or select plants that can withstand a good bit of foot traffic.

Wildlife Want insects and birds? The more diverse the plant palette the better.

Budget How deep are your pockets? All types of green roofs depend on proper preparation, installation, and long-term maintenance. Keep the financial scope of the system—including plant choices—in mind.

and access. To limit growth and root encroachment, growing large plants in containers is recommended (see "Rooftop Container Gardening," page 92).

Plants for Semi-intensive Systems Many green roofs are a hybrid of the two main systems. This might involve a combination of shallow areas that support groundcovers and berms of deeper soil that can support accent plants. Aim for a ratio of 80 percent groundcover plants to 20 percent accent specimens to ensure good year-round coverage, since many accent plants are seasonal. More groundcover also gives weeds less opportunity to establish themselves. Semi-intensive systems can also be good venues for encouraging biodiversity and attracting pollinators (although you can also do so with both extensive and intensive systems): Select a broad array of plant species and include high pollen- and nectar-producing plants like *Crocus*, *Delosperma*, and *Phemeranthus* species.

Site Conditions

Rooftops are usually harsh environments. Most endure extreme sun and heat as well as high winds, but others may be in deep shade if they stand in the shadow of neighboring buildings. Even more than ground-level gardens, roof garden conditions are highly individual. A skyscraper rooftop, for example, will experience much more extreme weather than one located on a three-story brownstone. A single roof can include various microclimates, too. Observing conditions over time will help you select the plants that will do best on your roof.

Starting the Garden

There are a number of ways to establish a green roof, and the method you choose will depend on your budget and timing.

Pregrown mats or modules, nursery-grown units in which the plants are fully mature at delivery, will create a roof garden almost immediately upon installation. Mats tend to be about one inch thick and roll out like sod. Because their soil layer is thin, they can only support sedums (although you can supplement them with plugs of other species). Green roof modules—trays of varying sizes and depths filled with plants—are also pregrown and produce instant results upon installation. The key difference is that mats are rolled out on top of the growing medium, while modules contain the medium and are placed over the root barrier layer. The main downside of both is their cost—these are the most expensive options.

Plugs, pregrown individual plants, allow you to expand beyond succulents into other perennials and grasses. They give much more design latitude, allowing you to vary textures and create drifts of color. Plugs are more costly than seeds or cuttings but less so than modules or mats. They are typically spaced two plants per square foot, which will usually spread to completely cover the bedding area in about a year. You can plant plugs more or less densely, depending on how fast you want the roof to fill in, but take the plant's mature size into consideration to avoid overcrowding. You can also plant them in combination with seeding or cutting.

Direct seeding onto the roof's soil is a low-cost option, but it's a slower way to establish your planting, and you have less control over the design unless you plant just one species. Also, there may be an initial period during which the roof is bare if your installation date is at odds with their germination season. Species that can be readily sown by seed include *Allium, Ipomopsis,* and *Phemeranthus.* Check the plants' germination requirements before buying seeds to be sure that their growing needs align with your growing conditions. After spreading the seeds, rake them into the media. Water promptly to ensure that they don't blow away. Seeding is not recommended on rooftops that are consistently exposed to high winds unless you're prepared to take precautionary measures: spraying the seeded soil with a hydromulch (a mix of water and shredded paper) or anchoring it with netting and keeping it moist.

Cuttings, while more costly than seeds, are another inexpensive way to establish plants. However, this approach is largely limited to succulents, since they are the only roof-appropriate plants that will readily root this way. Start succulent cuttings in spring to give them time to send out roots before blooming. Cuttings must stay

Pregrown mats (left) mature at the nursery and are rolled out on-site to provide a fully established roof. Plugs (right) are planted individually, which allows some design latitude.

in contact with the growing medium to root and must be adhered in some fashion, such as with a tackifier (a liquid resin that binds them to the soil), jute mesh, or hydromulch.

Maintaining a Green Roof

There's no such thing as a maintenance-free green roof. Even an extensive system with succulent groundcovers in shallow, nonirrigated media will need to be watered and weeded dilligently until the plants are fully established. And the more growing media, water, and organic material you use, the more likely that airborne weed seeds will invade. You should also expect more maintenance if your roof has a complex design that includes open space, a distinct pattern, or particular groupings.

No matter how carefully you plan, not all species will be equally long-lived, and plants will rise and fall from season to season and year to year. All green roof systems have open and bare areas at some point in the year. In the summer's heat and dryness, for example, some plants go dormant and rebound again in the fall. Other plants may need to be cut back to reduce the risk of fire. And if at some point the plantings are disturbed because the roof below needs work, you'll need to replace the plants that were removed using new plants or transplants from elsewhere on the roof. You can also reseed the spots or just let other plants fill in unaided over time.

Can species native to the Northeast, like black-eyed Susan (*Rudbeckia hirta*), thrive on a green roof? Researchers are testing these and other species for suitability.

Going Native?

Edward Toth and Matthew I. Palmer

Many people assume that plant species native to the New York area wouldn't perform as well on rooftops as the sedums that have become the go-to choices. But the truth is, there hasn't been any systematic attempt to find out—until now. The New York City Department of Parks and Recreation and Columbia University have embarked on a five-year project to study the performance of natives in green roof systems. Experiments using species from two different plant communities native to our region—the Hempstead Plains and the Rocky Summit Grassland—are under way right now.

Both environments—a natural prairie that was once expansive on Long Island and the open clearings found on the summits of northeastern mountains—are similar to green roofs in that they are drought prone, exposed to high winds and intense sunlight, and have shallow soil. For our initial investigation, launched in 2010, we chose eight representative species from each community and planted them in experimental plots on the rooftops of ten Parks Department recreation centers across the five boroughs. We'll put them through the paces and see which ones survive and reproduce, and monitor the complexity of the ecosystems that develop. What types of soil microbes arrive? Which insects do they attract? Since natives provide vital resources for local pollinators, we will also investigate whether native-planted green roofs can provide ecological linkages between larger natural areas like parks and other protected lands.

We'll be growing all our plants in both four- and six-inch-deep growing media. Most New York City green roofs are retrofits on older buildings, which means weight load (and consequently, soil depth) is often a limiting factor, so we need to consider shallow systems. In addition, we'll be measuring evapotranspiration rates—an essential function for green roofs. Native grasses and herbs may be more efficient than sedums in this respect. If so, native-based systems may be adopted more widely in the future.

We want to expand the range of green roof plants beyond the small number of genera and species currently in wide use. In the near future, we plan to study the suitability of up to 75 natives that we feel are good candidates for use on green roofs by submitting them to a series of controlled greenhouse tests. We'll then be able to provide landscapers and building owners with a suite of options, including detailed performance data that will take the guesswork out of choosing rooftop natives.

In the meantime, the Parks Department's Greenbelt Native Plant Center has an online list of native species that are good candidates (see "For More Information," page 102). Though these plants have not been vigorously tested in green roof systems yet, they are all good candidates for anyone ready to give natives a try.

Rooftop Container Gardening
Meredith Ford

Even if you lack the resources or the space to install a full intensive or extensive green roof system, you can still green your rooftop with container plantings. With advance planning, careful plant selection, and a commitment to maintenance and dirty work, do-it-yourselfers can create rooftop gardens that provide outdoor havens for themselves and their neighbors while fostering local wildlife, mitigating storm-water runoff, and contributing to urban sustainability.

First Things First

It goes without saying that in order to grow a roof garden, you must have a roof. But many city dwellers either rent or own an apartment in a shared building, and roof rights are not always included. Before you do anything else, be sure to check with your landlord, co-op board, condo organization, or building superintendent to determine what, if any, roof access you are granted.

If you skip this step and try to surreptitiously plant containers on your roof, you are likely to regret it. An angry landlord or super may drag all your hard work to the dumpster—or worse, you may find yourself liable for damage or injury.

At the same time, learn as much as you can about the roof's general condition as well as any upcoming maintenance requirements. This may be the year your roof is scheduled for repainting, for example. You don't want to invest in expensive and hard-to-move planters or other structures that the roofers would have to clear away. (See "Container Garden Checklist," page 95, for other matters to consider.)

Site Considerations

Once you've secured your roof space, you will need to assess the site just as you would when establishing a ground-level garden. You'll also want to plan how to address various site challenges.

Sun and Heat Make note of the site's light exposure. Most roofs receive full sun (more than six hours of direct sunlight a day), but if yours is shaded by neighboring buildings most of the day, you'll be better off growing shade-loving plants. If your roof is painted black, it will be significantly hotter than a white or silver roof—black

A rooftop container garden is a low-budget, do-it-yourself alternative for greening a rooftop. Potted plants host pollinators, absorb rainwater, and can even augment the dinner table.

roofs in New York City can reach 170°F on a very hot day—and you'll need plants that can survive such scorching temperatures.

Water Supply and Drainage During the growing season, most rooftop container plants need daily watering, so a rooftop water supply is essential. Many gardeners use drip irrigation fed from roof-level spigots because of the intense watering needs of wind- and sun-exposed roof plants. If there's no spigot, you could place a rooftop rain barrel on your roof, but before you do, take into account the weight of a full cistern, find a secure place to put it, and clear it with your landlord or coop board.

If neither of these is an option, you may be left to haul watering cans up from your apartment. If so, it might be impractical to grow more than a few plants. Of course, succulents and other drought-resistant plants can go longer between watering and thus lighten your workload. No matter what type of plants you use, plan to place rubber mats, wooden decking, or some other buffer beneath your containers to help them drain more efficiently and protect roofing materials.

Wind It can be extremely gusty on a roof, especially if it's unshielded by adjacent buildings. Take note of the areas that are most vulnerable to wind and plan accordingly. If your roof has no windbreaks, either install something to shelter your plants—like a well-secured trellis—or choose low containers that hug the perimeter

Low wooden planters are a good bet for windy rooftops. Placing them alongside the wall of an adjacent building or another other fixed structure also helps keep them sheltered.

Container Garden Checklist

After you've received the okay to set up a garden on your roof—and before you rush to the garden center to buy new containers and plants—here are a few logistical matters you should attend to.

- The weight of your roof garden—pots, soil, growing plants—is a crucial issue. If your design is fairly ambitious—say you want to include trees or large containers— consult an engineer or a landscape professional who specializes in roof gardens to determine the stability of your roof. (See "The Feasibility Study," page 81.)

- If your roof is sloped, a professional contractor must create a flat space for you to garden on (which will likely require a permit).

- Your roof must have a functioning drain—you'll be adding to the roof's runoff as you water your containers.

- If your ideal roof garden includes a deck, pergola, storage shed, or other fixed structure, determine whether or not city or local ordinances restrict your building rights on the roof. You may need to apply for a permit.

- Local fire codes likely govern the use of roof space. Plan for clear pathways throughout the space and maintain easy access to the roof's door and/or fire escapes.

- If children will be enjoying your roof garden with you, a safety railing should be installed.

walls. (Intake fans and air conditioning equipment are not good windbreaks to grow plants against—their heat output will scorch them and perhaps pose a fire hazard.)

Wind-catching plants like trees are likely to topple over in high winds, especially if they're planted in top-heavy, vase-shaped containers, so use square planters instead and position them against a windbreak. Unless they're well sheltered and staked, long-stemmed flowers will be battered, so consider growing shrubs and low-growing flowering plants instead. Lightweight lawn chairs, gardening materials, watering cans and tools are liable to take flight in windy weather (and possibly injure someone in the process), so be sure to completely secure all your rooftop furnishings and supplies.

Soils and Planters No matter what you intend to plant, lightweight growing medium is a must for any rooftop garden to help reduce its overall load. Bagged soils marketed as container mixes, available at garden supply stores, tend to contain sphagnum, perlite, and vermiculite, which are lighter than garden soil and also help retain moisture and provide aeration.

Look for plastic or lightweight wooden planters and pots rather than heavier terra-cotta or concrete ones. Commercial sub-irrigated planters like EarthBoxes can be an especially useful option for rooftops. Also called self-watering planters, they contain reservoirs that can help stretch the time between watering.

Think outside the pot. Rooftop plants can grow well in inexpensive (or free) repurposed containers of all sorts. This plastic tote bag has the added benefit of being very lightweight.

Budget-conscious roof gardeners can make their own planters out of wide range of repurposed receptacles like children's wading pools, plastic buckets, and recycling bins with holes drilled in the bottom for drainage. Some gardeners even have good luck with old coffee cans or heavy-duty plastic shopping bags. For vertical plantings, consider trellises, pergolas, or commercial hanging systems, like Woolly Pockets, that can be installed on walls.

Plant Selection, Maintenance, and Design Intent

Once you've assessed your roof site and planned your approach, the fun begins: You can now choose your plants. Drought- and heat-tolerant plants are most likely to do well in windy and dry rooftop conditions, but you needn't stick to low-growing succulents. To a large extent, learning which plants are most successful on your roof is a trial-and-error process. Almost anything, aside from large trees that demand extensive space for rooting, can grow well in a container, but your particular site conditions will play a large part in determining which plants grow successfully there. Here are some things to keep in mind.

Birds, Bees, and Natives Consider growing drought-tolerant species native to your region. Native plants are prime attractors for local wildlife, so even the most humble rooftop container garden can become a habitat for local pollinators and birds. Veteran roof gardener Ellen Spector Platt, who presides over a garden of more than 75 containers on the roof of her Manhattan high-rise apartment building, frequently spots butterflies, songbirds, and pollinating moths flitting through her garden—18 stories above street level. At the same time, Platt, who was once in charge of a five-acre farm in Pennsylvania, appreciates how the location protects her garden from unwanted predators. "Up on the roof, you never have to worry about deer nibbling your plants," she says.

Trees and Shrubs Many small ornamental trees and shrubs like river birch (*Betula nigra*), serviceberries (*Amelanchier* species), and Japanese maple (*Acer palmatum*) do quite well in rooftop gardens if they're planted in large, stable containers and protected from the wind. This will add substantial weight, however, so be sure to determine whether or not your roof can bear it before you invest the effort and expense. After a few years you may need to do some root trimming to keep your plants to a manageable size.

Weeds and Pests Plan on dedicating some time in the warm months to weeding and deadheading. Check your plants carefully for insect pests and diseases—early detection can help you avoid the need for chemical intervention. Beware that windy rooftops are often host to volunteer plants—mugwort, clover, or even a feral maple may try to establish themselves in your containers. Remove dead leaves and other detritus before they clog your roof's drain.

One key environmental benefit of a rooftop container garden is that it can provide resources for bees and other pollinators in places where habitat and food sources are scarce.

Winter Protection Just as rooftops are harsher climates than ground-level gardens in spring, summer, and fall, they can be extremely bleak environments during the winter. Do some research to find out what your plants will need for winter protection. Some smaller plants can be brought inside, and large perennials should be winterized with extra mulch. Woody vines and shrubs like American wisteria (*Wisteria frutescens*) and arborvitae (*Thuja* species), as well as containerized trees like Japanese maple (*Acer palmatum*), flowering plum (*Prunus triloba*), and river birch (*Betula nigra*), usually overwinter well with protective wrappings of burlap or plastic.

Edibles Sunny rooftops can be great spots to grow edible plants. Many vegetables, herbs, and fruits are annuals, so you can try different varieties and cultivars each year. They're also great plants to share with your neighbors. Roof gardener Platt cultivates a "pinch an inch" patch of lettuces and herbs and invites everyone in her building to collect from it.

One year she grew peanuts, much to the amazement and education of the city-dwelling children in her building, who had never conceived that this snack food comes from a plant. Anything you grow to eat on your rooftop should be carefully washed beforehand: Just like streetside and backyard urban gardens, urban rooftops—particularly those near major roadways—receive airborne pollution.

Entertaining You don't need a lot of space to create a container garden worthy of guests. Brooklyn roof gardener Chris Phillips keeps about 15 containers—from small pots of coleus to huge planters containing large evergreen shrubs—on a 6-by-12-foot common roof deck atop his coop building. Many of Phillips's neighbors hold cock-

The Buzz on Urban Beekeeping

Interested in raising honey bees on your roof? You're in good company. Rooftop beekeeping is on the rise in many cities, including New York, where the practice was recently legalized. Most cities require hives to be registered, but once you've taken that simple step, resources abound. Local groups like the New York City Beekeepers Association, the San Francisco Beekeepers Association, and the Chicago Honey Co-op offer guidance for getting started. There are also smaller beekeeping groups around the country that organize via Meetup.com. The magazines *Bee Culture* and the *American Bee Journal* are also great resources for beginners.

Ellen Spector Platt's sunny Manhattan rooftop garden produces enough salad greens and herbs that she's happy to share her bounty with her neighbors.

tail parties and cookouts in the garden, which includes a dining table and chairs, so his focus is on creating a space for evening enjoyment. To that end, he avoids edible plants and instead grows decorative ones, especially those with white flowers that are visible to nighttime visitors. Phillips has also had success with fragrant plants like lavender and roses.

Roof gardens are a great way to draw people together, whether you're the sole owner and use it for hosting guests or live in a shared building with dozens of tenants. Even a small number of plants on the roof can transform an otherwise barren space into an outdoor oasis. Add some solar lanterns, a deck chair or two, and a picnic table, and you may find you never want to descend the stairs back to your indoor home.

Bringing a Green Roof to Your School

Elizabeth Peters

Installing a green roof on any existing building requires serious commitment, careful planning, and a clear vision. Anytime the building is not your own, you'll have extra legwork in store, and when the project involves a city-owned building and the safety of schoolchildren, the amount of work can seem daunting. Don't let that scare you away. Moving forward on such a project will take teamwork, time, and effort, but it is within your grasp. Below are some tips to get you started on a green roof on a public school or other shared building.

Think of the end at the beginning. This is a big project, so it's crucial to have a clear goal. Envision your ideal completed project, but be prepared to circle back and make adjustments to the design and implementation of your plan.

Articulate your vision. It often helps to write out, in the present tense, a description of your green roof to be. What does it look like? Who gets to enjoy it? What benefits does it offer? Use the profiles in this book as a launching point.

Learn from veterans. Visit schools with green roofs and talk to the people who made them happen. They can point you to resources specific to your project. For example, the NYC School Construction Authority posts comprehensive instructions for submitting applications, feasibility reports, and other materials (nysca.org).

Assemble a team. Enlist school parents, teachers, administrators, and other interested parties. Assemble a list of professionals who may be helpful down the road, as well as contacts at your local department of education, department of buildings, and school construction authority. Keep key players informed with monthly updates through an electronic mailing list or social media group. Develop an administrative steering committee and subcommittees to focus on specific tasks like fundraising and curriculum development.

Keep the team engaged. Try to avoid open-ended responsibilities and instead assign specific tasks, like making an introduction, researching a topic, or attending a meeting. As the project moves into production, stakeholders can help with tasks like starting plants at home and attending workdays for installation and maintenance. Even if you don't actually need such volunteer assistance, giving your supporters something concrete to do helps cement their relationship with the project.

Craft a mission statement and an "elevator pitch." Zero in on the top three reasons for your project, and use them as the basis for both. The mission statement should describe your purpose in fairly formal language. The elevator pitch conveys similar information but in a conversational and sometimes personal way: In a conversation as short as an elevator ride, you should be able to spark someone's interest and desire to learn more.

Design a sharp-looking proposal. The first draft may be simply your mission statement, a compelling photo, and your contact information. Later editions may include the full suite of your project plans, supporting articles about green roofs, letters of support, and so on. At all stages, your proposal should convey both your group's professionalism and the excitement surrounding the project. Retrofits rarely pay for themselves quickly or directly with cost savings, so your proposal needs to stress other ways to evaluate its worth.

Break your budget into stages. Your budget will depend on the building's current condition and the scale and goals of the project. Start with your best guesses for costs, get feedback from folks familiar with projects like yours, and revise as necessary. You can use such ballpark figures for early proposals, but you'll likely hire a professional estimator to prepare a budget suitable for applications. Don't forget to include these items:

- **Research:** photocopies, phone calls, transportation, entertainment, etc.

- **Feasibility study** (see page 81).

- **Fundraising:** grant-writing fees, fundraising events, copies of the proposal and other materials, etc.

- **Preconstruction:** fees for the architect, landscape designer, and other professionals, plus the costs of putting projects out to bid.

- **Construction:** installation of the green roof system itself, plus pathways, fencing, etc. Also factor in the costs of any repairs to your existing roof, construction permits, and fixes for any building code violations.

- **Installation:** delivery and installation of growing medium, plant matter, irrigation systems, etc.

- **Maintenance:** annual costs of maintaining the roof, replacing plants, etc.

Do a feasibility study early. Your first fundraising goal should be to pay for this, as the engineer may uncover information that requires you to modify your original plans or conditions that you will need to remediate prior to construction. Be sure to research the type of report that will be required later for permits.

Define the use of the roof. If your roof will function as a classroom, you will need to get a new certificate of occupancy—meaning your project will need to comply with building codes related to accessibility, safety, and egress. If the roof will be used only as a demonstration area, you may be exempt from some requirements.

Don't miss opportunities to "fundraise" by saving money. Take the time to research and apply not only for grants but also for incentives, abatements, and donated services. You can also hire a pro for this step.

Base your time line on seasonality. For example, summer break may be the best time of year to perform any school construction. The optimal planting windows are usually spring and fall. Keep in mind that nurseries may need up to 18 months of lead time to grow your plant material.

Enjoy your green roof and spread the word! Once it's installed, be sure to thank everyone who has helped with the project, and make them a part of your success. Share your new expertise with others to give them a head start on their own endeavors.

For More Information

GENERAL

Green Roofs for Healthy Cities
News, background, resources, and
information on the industry association's
green roof seminars and courses for North
American professionals and beginners.
greenroofs.org

Greenroofs.com
Industry news and profiles of recently
completed vegetated walls and roofs,
frequently updated.
greenroofs.com

Chicago Green Roofs
A how-to guide tailored to Chicago
residents but with broadly applicable
information.
chicagogreenroofs.org

ASLA Green Roof
Image galleries, virtual tours, and fact
sheets from the American Society of
Landscape Architects.
asla.org/greenroof

NATIVE PLANTS

**Greenbelt Native Plant Center
Green Roof Species List**
(Northeastern natives)
www.nycgovparks.org/greening/greenbelt-
native-plant-center/garden-species-lists/
garden-green-roof

**Lady Bird Johnson
Wildflower Center**
(Southwestern natives)
www.wildflower.org/greenroof

ROOFTOP FARMING

FarmingUp
farmingup.org

Eagle Street Rooftop Farm
rooftopfarms.org

Brooklyn Grange
brooklyngrangefarm.com

BOOKS

*The Green Roof Manual: A
Professional Guide to Design,
Installation, and Maintenancee*
Edmund C. Snodgrass and Linda McIntyre,
Timber Press, 2010

*Green Roof Construction and
Maintenance*
Kelly Luckett, McGraw-Hill, 2009

*Green Roof Plants: A Resource and
Planting Guide*
Edmund and Lucie Snodgrass,
Timber Press 2006

*Rooftop and Terrace Gardens: A Step
by Step Guide to Creating a Modern
and Stylish Space*
Caroline Tilston, John Wiley and Sons, 2008

*Planting Green Roofs and
Living Walls*
Nigel Dunnet and Noel Kingsbury, Timber
Press 2004

*Roof Gardens: History, Design and
Construction*
Theodore H. Osmundson, Norton, 1997

CONTAINER GARDENS

Blogs

Garden Bytes from the Big Apple
www.gardenbytes.com

Brooklyn Roof Garden
brooklynroofgarden.com

66 Square Feet
66squarefeet.blogspot.com

Manhattan Rooftop Garden
Project:
nycroofgardenproject.blogspot.com

Bucolic Bushwick
bucolicbushwick.com

Planters and Tools

Fire Escape Farms
fireescapefarms.com

EarthBox
earthbox.com

Woolly Pocket
woollypocket.com

SUPPLIERS

Emory Knoll Farms
greenroofplants.com

Jost Greenhouses
jostgreenhouses.com

SkyGarden Extensive and Intensive
Roof Media
stancills.com/skygarden

Rooflite
rooflitesoil.com

American Hydrotech
hydrotechusa.com

Green Roof Blocks
greenroofblocks.com

Tecta America
tectaamerica.com

LiveRoof
liveroof.com

GreenGrid Roofs
greengridroofs.com

ENERGY EFFICIENCY AND WATER MANAGEMENT

"A Temperature and Seasonal
Energy Analysis of Green, White,
and Black Roofs"
S.R. Gaffin, et al. Columbia University,
Center for Climate Systems Research,
accessed at http://www.coned.com/
coolroofstudy/

"Stormwater Retention for a
Modular Green Roof"
S.R. Gaffin, et al. Columbia University,
Center for Climate Systems Research,
accessed at www.coned.com/
greenroofcolumbia/

"Green Roofs for Stormwater
Runoff Control"
Robert D. Berghage, et al.
US Environmental Protection Agency,
National Risk Management Research
Laboratory, accessed at www.epa.gov/
nrmrl/pubs/600r09026/600r09026.pdf

"Reducing Urban Heat Islands:
Compendium of Strategies,
Green Roofs"
EPA Office of Atmospheric Programs,
accessed at www.epa.gov/heatisland/
resources/pdf/GreenRoofsCompendium.pdf

Contributors

Tracey Faireland is a professional engineer, licensed general contractor, and the director of Capital Projects at Brooklyn Botanic Garden, where she is overseeing the design and construction of projects within BBG's Campaign for the Next Century, including a LEED-certified Visitor Center, storm-water management system, and water conservation project.

Meredith Ford is a freelance writer and editor. She was formerly the editor of Brooklyn Botanic Garden's *Plants & Gardens News* and managing editor of BBG's online peer-reviewed science journal, *Urban Habitats*. She was the associate editor of BBG's guidebook *Edible Gardens* and attempts her own edible gardening in her Brooklyn backyard.

Beth Hanson is a former managing editor of Brooklyn Botanic Garden's handbook series and has edited 11 BBG handbooks, including *The Best Apples to Buy and Grow* and *Easy Compost*. She also contributed to BBG's *Gardener's Desk Reference* (Henry Holt, 1998) and writes about gardening, science, and health for various publications, including *Organic Gardening* magazine. She lives outside New York City, where she is a master gardener volunteer.

Haven Kiers is an accredited LEED (Leadership in Energy and Environmental Design) professional and founding partner of GreenSwell Design and Planning, a green infrastructure design firm. She writes for Greenroofs.com, is a trainer with Green Roofs for Healthy Cities, and teaches a course on green roofs at the University of California-Davis Extension.

Yessica Mariñez is a project associate at Rand Engineering & Architecture, where she leads the firm's green team, specializing in green roofs and other sustainable design projects. She holds professional accreditation with LEED and the Building Performance Institute. She also administered the first green roof installation at the Fashion Institute of Technology and is working with FIT on its second green roof.

Matthew I. Palmer is a botanist and faculty member in the Department of Ecology, Evolution, and Environmental Biology at Columbia University. His research interests are rooted in community ecology, with emphases on conservation, restoration, and ecosystem function, from which his research on green roofs extends.

Elizabeth Peters is the director of Digital and Print Media at Brooklyn Botanic Garden, where she publishes the Guides for a Greener Planet imprint and oversees the Garden's website, bbg.org. She also edited the BBG books *Edible Gardens*, *Community Gardening*, and *The Tree Book for Kids and Their Grown-ups*. As the former director of the Austin Film Society, Peters coached independent filmmakers on crafting proposals, fundraising, and collaboration on large creative projects.

Sarah Schmidt is an editor at Brooklyn Botanic Garden. She has also written about sustainability and urban issues for newspapers and magazines, including *OnEarth*, *The New York Times, New York Magazine*, and *Plenty*. She lives in Brooklyn, where she tends five window boxes and her co-op's backyard garden.

Edmund C. Snodgrass, a fifth-generation farmer and nurseryman, is president and founder of Emory Knoll Farms and Green Roof Plants. Snodgrass collaborates on green roof research with academic institutions and advises botanic gardens, including the Singapore Botanic Garden and the U.S. Botanic Garden, on green roof installations. He is the coauthor of *Green Roof Plants: A Resource and Planting Guide* (Timber Press, 2006), *The Green Roof Manual* (Timber Press, 2010), and *Small Green Roofs* (Timber Press, 2011).

Edward Toth is the director of the Greenbelt Native Plant Center, a 13-acre nursery, greenhouse, bulk-seed resource, and seed bank facility owned and operated by the New York City Department of Parks and Recreation. In addition to working toward the conservation of the region's native flora, Toth and his team began efforts in 2012 to organize a mid-Atlantic regional seed bank as part of the national Seeds of Success program.

Linda S. Velazquez is founder and publisher of Greenroofs.com, where she writes and reports about green roofs and walls. She is an associate member of the American Society of Landscape Architects, an accredited LEED professional, and an accredited green roof professional through Green Roofs for Healthy Cities. She is also principal of Sky Gardens Design, a green roof design and consulting firm in Alpharetta, Georgia.

PHOTOS

Laura Berman Pages 92, 96

Rebecca Bullene Page 74

Brooklyn Grange Page 15 (bottom)

Mark Bussell 38, 40

Cook + Fox Architects Page 4

Alan and Linda Detrick Page 99

Bilyana Dimitrova Page 25

Elizabeth Ennis Page 75

Peter I. Fifield Page 41 (left)

Ira Goldstein Page 6

New York Public Library Page 10

Elizabeth Peters Pages 2, 22, 24 (left, right), 42, 44, 45, 58 (top left, middle right), 62 (right), 67 (right), 68, 70 (right), 76, 90

Josef Pinlac Page 41 (right)

David Puchkoff Pages 46, 48 (left, right), 49

Sarah Schmidt Page 74 (right)

Julie C. Smith Page 86 (right)

Edmund C. Snodgrass Pages 14 (top), 86 (left), 89 (left, right)

Tara Thayer Cover, pages 14 (bottom), 15 (top), 20, 26. 28, 29 (left, right), 30, 32, 33 (left, right), 34, 36, 37 (left, right), 50, 52 (left, right), 53, 54, 56, 57, 58 (top right, middle left, bottom left, bottom right), 60, 62 (left), 63, 64, 66, 67 (left), 70 (left), 71, 79, 80, 83, 84, 94, 97, 98

Vancouver Board of Parks and Recreation Page 15 (third from top)

ILLUSTRATION

Elizabeth Ennis Page 18

Index

Promoting Organic and Sustainable Gardening

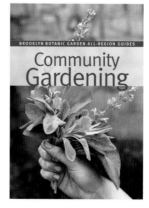

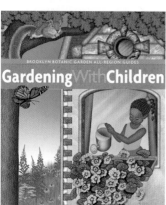

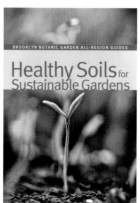

BBG Guides for a Greener Planet

World renowned for pioneering gardening information, Brooklyn Botanic Garden's award-winning guides provide practical advice in a compact format for gardeners across North America. To order other fine titles, shop online at bbg.org/handbooks or call 718-623-7280. To learn more about Brooklyn Botanic Garden, visit bbg.org.